The consultancy study was commissioned by the Forum
for Peace and Reconciliation. A first draft was presented to the Forum at
its meeting on 14 July 1995 and was finalized on 29 December 1995.
The views expressed are those of the authors and are not
necessarily those of the Forum or its members.
Publication, with an accompanying Forum commentary,
was authorized by the Forum's Coordinating Committee
on 15 December 1995, subject to final clearance by the
Economic Sub-Committee. In view of the continuing
deferral, since early February 1996, of meetings of the Forum
and of its committees, the study is now being published,
without the commentary, on the authority of the Chairperson
because of its relevance to the peace process and all-party
negotiations. It is hoped to publish the Forum commentary
at a later date.

We dedicate this work to the memories of Secretary Ron Brown and Assistant Secretary Charles Meissner, US Department of Commerce, who both died so tragically in Croatia on 3 April 1996. As men who 'fly in and out', they did indeed care a great deal, working tirelessly to promote peace and reconciliation throughout the world.

Charles Meissner addressed the Forum on Friday 16 December 1994.

TABLE OF CONTENTS

ACKNOWLEDGEMENTS

This study was commissioned by the Forum for Peace and Reconciliation with a brief to explore the long-term social and economic consequences of peace and reconciliation in the island of Ireland. A natural split can be made between the short-to medium-term matters that will accompany the peace process, over a time horizon of up to five years, and long-term issues that will become important over a time horizon extending out to about twenty years. The former issues were treated in an earlier report to the Forum, prepared by KPMG Management Consultants and others (KPMG 1995) and tend to be relatively concrete and specific. The latter issues are, by their very nature, more speculative and exploratory, and our report is as much designed to seek out and pose interesting and relevant questions as it is to provide concrete and definitive answers. Hence, the two reports are intended to be complementary and to be read in conjunction with each other.

The study draws extensively on results from North-South economic research work carried out at the Economic and Social Research Institute since the Autumn of 1992. A joint ESRI/NIERC research programme, The Two Economies of Ireland was generously supported by a grant from the International Fund for Ireland, with further support from the Irish business sector. This joint project represented one of the first serious and sustained attempts to facilitate the collaboration of economic researchers from both regions of Ireland for the purposes of studying problems and issues of mutual interest. We acknowledge this support gratefully both for the opportunity it gave us to explore the economic past and future of our island and for the facility it provided us to meet and share experiences with Northern colleagues.

We acknowledge the many individuals who helped our work with a certain degree of apprehension, given the possibly contentious nature of some aspects of our report.

Cross-border economic analysis is difficult to divorce from its complex and controversial political context. Honest differences of opinion and of interpretation in economic and political matters, which would pass with little reaction among European colleagues, can easily be misunderstood and give offence in a cross-border context. Hence, it is particularly important to stress the caveat that none of those acknowledged is in any way responsible for the use or interpretation that we have made of their published work, help or advice.

A major inspiration to our research was provided by Sir George Quigley through his insightful papers and addresses on North-South issues, where he challenges economists and business analysts to think about the potentials of our island in a radically new and constructive way. His active support of our cross-border research, his championing of the concepts of the Belfast-Dublin Economic Corridor and of the 'island' economy as a strategic focus of North-South cooperation, have encouraged us to be more ambitious and constructively provocative in our study than might otherwise have been the case.

Dr Paul Gorecki, Director of the Northern Ireland Economic Council (NIEC), commented on an early draft of the report and provided us with the results of his own research into the peace dividend for the North, together with his many insights into the opportunities and challenges that peace offers. Douglas Hamilton, also of the NIEC, commented in detail on early drafts and was the source of many hours of enjoyable discussion and constructive speculation on Ireland's future prospects. Invitations from the NIEC to attend a series of important conferences and lectures on Northern topics during 1995 are also gratefully acknowledged.

Professor Paul Teague, of the University of Ulster at Jordanstown, is one of Ireland's most innovative and challenging writers on the Northern economy and North-South issues. We have benefited greatly from his friendly assistance and authoritative guidance on many Northern issues. We also thank Maureen O'Reilly of the Northern Ireland Economic Research Centre (NIERC) for providing interim reports on her study of Northern Ireland exports, and for her assistance in interpreting these data.

In the course of our work we have benefited from discussions with many people, North and South: Shirley McCay, Development Officer with the North-West Region Cross-Border Group in Derry; Dr Seán McDonagh, Director of Dundalk

Regional College of Technology; Gerry Carroll, manager of the Regional Development Centre, Dundalk, who was kind enough to spend a day introducing us to some of the high-technology firms in the Centre's cross-border small-business incubator unit; and Margaret Andrews, Chief Executive, Newry & Mourne Enterprise Agency. The invitation we received from Feargal McCormack, Group Innovator, Enterprise Newry Ltd, to speak at the Newry-Dundalk Conference in June, 1995, gave us a fascinating insight into the difficulties of practical cross-border cooperation, reminding us of how little we economists actually know about how the real world functions!

Dr Marjorie Mowlam, MP, provided us with copies of her speeches on Northern Ireland and Labour Party position papers on wider aspects of the British economy. Michael D'Arcy, of D'Arcy Smyth and Associates, gave us detailed comments on an early draft of the report and provided many insights into North-South business opportunities through our participation in his path-breaking *Border Crossings* book project, jointly edited by Michael and by Tim Dickson. Bob Curran, of the Department of Finance, gave us the benefit of his reflections on the nature of the Northern subvention after an earlier presentation of some of our results to the Statistical and Social Inquiry Society. Jim Mongey, of An Bórd Tráchtála, provided us with advice and information on recent cross-border trade initiatives. Peter McGregor and Brian Ashcroft, of the Fraser of Allander Institute, University of Strathclyde, shared with us their Scottish-based insights into Ireland's region problems; Noel Farley, of Bryn Mawr College, Pennsylvania, helped us through his research into the performance of Northern and Southern manufacturing industry. Mary Bradley, our sternest critic, read earlier drafts of the report from the point of view of a non-economist, and assisted in tracking down and eliminating the worst examples of our impenetrable jargon.

At the Economic and Social Research Institute, research assistance on this project was provided by Nuala O'Donnell, Colm O'Reardon and Niamh Sheridan. My colleagues Denis Conniffe and Joanne McCartan read and commented on early drafts of the report, and John FitzGerald provided invaluable advice on reform of the CAP. Our heavy demands for access to publications on North-South issues were efficiently handled by the Institute's librarian, Maura Rohan, and library assistant, Regina Costello, who have become expert in securing documents from the most obscure of sources.

Finally, Walter Kirwan, Secretary-General of the Forum for Peace and Reconciliation, together with members of the Forum Secretariat, helped us improve the draft report immeasurably through providing detailed sets of their own perceptive and searching comments, criticisms and suggestions, and through processing the comments of the Forum delegations. We learned much from this process and are grateful to the Secretariat and to all the delegations for their meticulous care and attention and the interest they showed at the formal presentation of the draft report to a meeting of the Forum held on 10 November 1995.

Needless to say, all interpretations and any remaining errors and omissions are our responsibility since it would be unreasonable in a study as wide-ranging as this to expect complete agreement on all points. Although the author is employed at the Economic and Social Research Institute, Dublin, the Institute is not responsible for either the content or the views expressed in this report. Such responsibility rests with the author alone.

1. INTRODUCTION

1.1 BACKGROUND

The cessation of paramilitary violence in Northern Ireland from October 1994 removed a major constraint on the normal conduct of life on this island, both North and South.[1] This welcome development has generated interest in the study of how the violence of the last twenty five years (the troubles) may have hindered growth, diminished welfare and influenced structural change in both economies.[2] The advent of peace has also stimulated research into the nature of other constraints on island-wide growth and the extent to which their relaxation could have future beneficial economic consequences in the short, medium and long terms. Indeed, the prospect of positive peace dividends, both of a social and economic kind, is likely to be an important factor in preserving and consolidating the peace.

At the present time of peace in the North, with an understandably heightened awareness of Northern political and economic policy developments, it is easy to forget how much of the public discussion of the two economies of Ireland is a very recent phenomenon. Limited communication between Northern and Southern researchers over the years had led to a widespread lack of knowledge about parts of our island. It is easy to see why this happened. Northern researchers tended to look to Britain and often placed the economy of Northern Ireland purely in the context of British regions, generally ignoring the Republic of Ireland (e.g., Harris 1991). Southern researchers, on the other hand, tended to be more preoccupied with the role of the Southern economy in the European and world contexts, where separate treatment of Northern Ireland tended to be swamped by a more dominant concern with the British or aggregate UK economy (e.g., Cantillon et al. 1994).

1

Happily, the previous absence of collaborative interaction is coming to an end and over wide areas of economics, sociology, business and policy-making, Northern and Southern researchers, policy analysts and policy-makers are discovering common interests that spring from many shared experiences and the expectation of mutual benefits from deepening cross-border interchanges. Projects supported by the International Fund for Ireland and other private sector initiatives, together with the activities of the Forum for Peace and Reconciliation and of the EU (such as INTERREG and the EU Initiative for Peace and Reconciliation), now mean that remarkably generous encouragement is being given to cross-border interactions, involving review and exploration of every aspect of life on this island.

Given our understandable preoccupation with present day North-South economic problems and challenges, the fact is sometimes overlooked that even if the most recent Northern troubles had never broken out in 1969, the economies of both North and South would have faced serious challenges in coping with, and adjusting to, change in the latter half of the twentieth century. There can be little shelter or protection for small and peripheral nations and regions from the competitive forces generated by larger more powerful economies in a world of rapid technological progress, increasingly integrated global markets and shifts in the international division of labour. Small economies must perform to the very best international standards and exploit fully all their limited domestic advantages if they are to share the high standard of living enjoyed, for example, by the wealthier EU member States or by the wealthier regions of these States.[3]

From the 1950s the Northern economy faced serious adjustment problems, irrespective of the additional complications caused by the troubles in the late 1960s. In particular, there was an urgent need to accelerate the process of restructuring and diversification away from industries that had formed the core of its phenomenally successful nineteenth century growth, mainly shipbuilding, linen, and their associated engineering activities. Nor was the situation in the South any less challenging. An overriding necessity was the modernization of the inefficient, slow-growing, inward-oriented manufacturing sector that had been heavily protected behind tariff barriers since the early 1930s, and its reorientation towards export markets and higher quality products.

Within each of the two regions of the island there were economic black-spots which had missed out on whatever prosperity there was in Ireland of the late 1950s.

Although aggregate unemployment rates were low by modern standards, there was much local and unrecorded unemployment and under-employment. Furthermore, both regions, but particularly the South, had suffered a population haemhorrage through emigration that continued into the mid-twentieth century a pattern established mainly during and after the Great Famine of the mid-nineteenth century. In addition, both regions had severe limits on the amount of public sector resources available to promote development, stemming from binding sovereign borrowing limits in the South and the traditionally parsimonious behaviour of the UK Treasury in the North, where some semblance of fiscal self-sufficiency was required of the North by the UK public authorities at Westminster.

This already complex and challenging set of restructuring problems was seriously exacerbated by the eruption of violence in the North in the late 1960s. An immediate economic casualty in both regions was tourism, which was heavily dependent on the British market: for example, numbers of British visitors to the South collapsed and the real level of Southern earnings from tourism in 1968 was not to be reached again for twenty years. A similar collapse occurred in numbers visiting the North (Tansey 1995). The task of attracting foreign direct investment (FDI) to the North became ever more difficult, and although Britain continued to be the major source of inward investment, British firms provided a declining share of total manufacturing employment (39 per cent in 1973, but only 22 per cent in 1990). In contrast, the major share of FDI and their associated jobs in the South was provided by the United States, with Britain playing an important but lesser role.

A sizeable fraction of inward investment in the North during the 1960s and 1970s was in mature sectors such as textiles and artificial fibres, and was attracted mainly by high subsidies and the presence of other associated traditional activities in these areas. However, these new petroleum-based industries proved particularly vulnerable to the massive oil price rises of the 1970s, which precipitated major closures and job losses. As Northern manufacturing contracted, the public sector grew, bringing pressure on regional public expenditure at a time when the local tax base was shrinking. After the proroguing of Stormont and the imposition of direct rule in 1972, any remaining pretence of Northern financial self-sufficiency vanished, and a rapidly rising level of direct subvention was required to keep the region's economy afloat.

Many of the pressures on the North had direct and indirect parallels in the South. The onset of the world recessions, associated with the OPEC I and II oil price crises during the mid-1970s and early 1980s, ushered in a period of much slower and unstable world growth, with a consequent slackening in the world supply of mobile direct investment. As traditional indigenous industries declined, the ability of the South to continue to attract a high proportion of the available inward investment, in particular from the US, contrasted sharply with the difficulties faced by the North. However, not all the differences in North-South behaviour were due to the troubles, since there were crucial policy differences in the means available to attract inward investment.[4]

A pattern of public sector growth and increased public sector indebtedness similar to that in the North took place in the South from the mid-1970s, but was eventually choked off and reversed from the mid-1980s, although it has shown a tendency to grow again in more recent years.[5] Here, the implications of the status of the North as a region within the UK contrasted strongly with the obligations of sovereign independence in the South, where pressures for fiscal restructuring simply could not be ignored or passed on completely, or in large part, to a higher-level funding authority. Although the interpretation of the economic impact of the Southern public sector expansion and subsequent fiscal restructuring of the late 1980s is an area of some controversy, nevertheless there are interesting lessons to be drawn from this experience that may apply to the North, should it wish or need to move towards the restoration of greater regional balance within the UK.

The behaviour of the Northern and Southern economies from the 1960s to the present date is obviously of fundamental relevance to the analysis of the immediate social and economic consequences of an era of peace. At the very least, any evaluation or quantification of the costs of the past troubles could provide insights into the likely future benefits of peace. However, since the troubles lasted for over twenty five years, their costs and the most effective unwinding and reversal of these costs are very unlikely to be symmetrical.

Many reasons for a likely lack of symmetry could be advanced. For example, the passing of time and the consequences of violence during the past twenty five years seldom involved merely variations in the rate of capacity *utilization* of existing manufacturing plants and businesses. Rather, individual plants and whole sectors were damaged, diminished irreparably or simply ceased trading altogether. The offsetting massive growth of the Northern public sector has brought about heavy dependence by the Northern private sector on direct State support of questionable efficiency or indirect support through public demand for goods and services that may prove difficult to unwind. Furthermore, skilled emigrants, who left during the earlier years of the violence, have developed lives elsewhere and will not always return. More seriously, young people who have grown up in the North during the past twenty five years may have had their economic life-chances permanently impaired by exposure to violence.

Thus, some of the effects of the troubles on the Northern economy may be characterized by hysteresis, i.e., a situation where any initial deterioration caused by an adverse shock has a tendency to endure, and neither individuals, firms, sectors nor the overall economy can be guaranteed to bounce back after the original negative pressures are removed. Nor is the peace process likely to be a zero-sum game over the full twenty five year cycle of peace-violence-peace. The benefits of recovery and reconstruction could be less than, equal to, or greater than the damage caused by the protracted violence, depending on world economic conditions and domestic policy choices made in response to the peace.

The point at issue here is that the cessation of violence is just one of many factors influencing the two economies of the island and, in the case of the South, certainly not the major factor. For example, the consequences of peace during a world economic boom would be quite different from the consequences during a world recession. Similarly, the consequences of peace in an island where North and South continue in separate or back-to-back economic development is likely to differ greatly from a situation of North-South economic and business policy rapprochement. Hence, economic forces and institutions on the island need to be explored in the widest possible historical, political and social framework, in addition to examining them in the context of a narrow focus on immediate economic changes associated with the transition to peace.

The present study, however, proposes to go further than an investigation of the recent past and forecast of the immediate future. No matter how important we deem the events of the last twenty five years to be, a much longer time horizon is needed in order to understand the historical socio-economic processes that operated on this island, and which led to the very different economic development experiences of North and South. The violence that escalated after 1968, and the economic damage it wrought, did not take place in a vacuum. Rather, the unfolding of events was conditioned by political, cultural, and socio-economic factors inherited from the past. We need a better understanding of these factors if we wish to talk about possible future prospects for an island economy.

To understand the challenges and opportunities that the advent of peace may be opening up for the economies of North and South, we need to take a very long time horizon, both to examine the past and to envisage the future. This might be thought somewhat unusual in a mainly economic study, since economists tend to place greater emphasis on short-term analysis and forecasting against a background of fixed institutions, specific policy assumptions and a hypothesized external environment. Within any such conventional short-term analytical framework the future seldom deviates more than marginally from the past. Quantitative projections can be run mechanically out into the future, but they almost never capture crucial turning points or the consequences of radical new departures in public policy or private sector behaviour.

Although we will focus mainly on economic issues in our long-term investigation, we are fully aware of the dangers inherent in any simplistic claim that economic factors predetermine political choices, or are even influential aspects of such choices.[6] What we wish to investigate, however, is the extent to which past economic developments on this island were influenced by such forces as technology, geography, factor endowments, demography, economic and social forces external to the island, or indeed by pure chance. The predominantly political-historical tradition of much research and writing on island developments has tended to down-play these economic aspects.[7] Furthermore, some influential studies may be biased by political points of view, as in the nationalist economic histories of the early part of the twentieth century.[8] Formulation of future economic policies will be enhanced by a better understanding of the island economy's historical experience, an appreciation of the extent to which events are often determined by factors barely under policy control, and the isolation of those crucial areas where domestic policy can indeed enhance competitive advantage. Seamus Deane (1984) puts this more philosophically when he says:

> We stand in servitude to history if we insist on it as an explanation for the future we might have had but won't have. Freeing ourselves from that, we can begin to anticipate, not remember our future.

1.2 OUTLINE STRUCTURE OF THE STUDY

Our study was written to complement a previous report commissioned by the Forum for Peace and Reconciliation that focused on the economic and social implications of peace over the remaining five years of this decade (KPMG 1995). Within that time horizon, even on a scenario of generally acceptable political settlement, the coordination of policies and the harmonization or amalgamation of North-South economy-related institutions is unlikely to reach all of the potential suggested by the Joint Framework Document of the Irish and British Governments. In this context, the Forum considered that a study with a time horizon of, say, ten to twenty five years would be of value. Such a study was designed to explore the potential effects of a more dynamic situation in which time would be available to permit, if agreed, extensive harmonization of economic policies applying in the South and in the North, coupled with development of cross-border or all-Ireland institutions, with whatever powers, executive or otherwise, would be necessary effectively to achieve objectives across a wide range of economic areas. In the preceding sentence, the words if agreed are vitally important; for the purposes of this study, it is fully accepted that any harmonization of economic policies or any developments of cross-border or all-Ireland institutions could only emerge as part of one or more agreements consented to by the people of Ireland, North and South.

Our study is divided into three main parts. Part I, comprising chapters 2 and 3, discusses the past history of the island economies. Part II, comprising chapters 4 and 5, explores future policy structures and wider economic issues that will heavily influence the performance of the island economies, irrespective of whatever North-South political settlements are reached. Part III, comprising chapters 6 and 7, explores possible consequences of policy choices and world developments for the economies of North and South, selecting specific combinations from those outlined in part II. A brief survey of economic research findings on the island economies, North and South, is presented in the Appendix, and a comprehensive bibliography concludes the study.

Since our main concern is with the economic future of the island of Ireland, the inclusion of the historical material discussed in part I requires some explanation. In chapter 2 we take a very brief historical overview of the island economy over the period 1750-1960, i.e., from the time when the first aspects of what we would now recognize as a modern Irish economy emerged in the early stages of the British industrial revolution, to the period just before the outbreak of the Northern troubles. This long perspective is not an irrelevant academic indulgence. On the contrary, it is probably only a slight exaggeration to claim that many of the key characteristics of the two regional economies of the island of Ireland in the mid-twentieth century were clearly discernible by the middle of the nineteenth century. The subsequent political consequences of this earlier period of demographic disruption and regionally skewed economic development were enormous, and facilitated the partition of the island economy in 1921. In spite of more recent changes, many key features of that mid-nineteenth century island economy still coexist with more recent developments.

Chapter 3 focuses on the 1960-94 period, during which both regions attempted to break with past patterns of development that had their origins in the nineteenth century. Here we restrict our analysis to narrower socio-economic issues, having previously outlined the broader historical-economic framework. We examine the evolution of both Northern and Southern economies as they reacted to external world events (the OPEC crises, the evolution of the European Union, etc.) and to internal socio-economic, demographic and political pressures. In particular, we focus on a few key issues: the behaviour of the private sector (mainly manufacturing, but including agriculture and market services); the growth of the public sector; labour market and demographic developments; public finance problems; competitiveness, trade and North-South interactions; and how attempts have been made to estimate the 'costs' of the troubles.

The legacy of history, combined with the lessons of the recent troubles, places both regions of Ireland in a position where some new beginnings are both necessary and feasible if peace endures. Subject to the usual caveats about external world circumstances, both regions seem set to enjoy better than average economic growth, even in the absence of any change in, or intensification of, North-South economic interactions. In chapter 4 we explore the notion of economic governance in the island of Ireland, a matter that requires examination of the relationship between the concept of 'natural economic zones' and existing national boundaries.

By economic governance we mean that subset of the totality of all aspects of policy in the two regions of this island that are concerned with purely economic issues. Of course it is completely artificial to separate out economic aspects of governance, and we do so in the full knowledge they are almost certainly inseparable from the wider political aspects. However, since it is our desire to expand economic thinking about the future of the island economy, our approach represents merely the first stage of an iterative process, requiring continual re-examination in the light of evolving political institutions and structures. One must break into this circular process with whatever means available and in this report we do so by means of economics.

Within our treatment of economic governance on this island we examine three possible evolutionary scenarios: continuing separate economic development, in which little or no proactive North-South policy or business cooperation takes place; cooperative economic development, in which some degree of progress is made in designing island policy frameworks and a business environment that are to the advantage of both regions; and a single island economy, being a specifically Irish version of complete economic and monetary union (EMU) for the entire island. In each case we identify key features of economic policy, and explore likely economic consequences.

The matters explored in chapter 5 concern the wider range of influences in addition to domestic public policy structures that need to be taken into account when considering the future of the two economies on this island. We take up three main themes.

The first theme relates to enterprise and industrial policy. In small open regions (like the North) and small open economies (like the South), the 'engine' of growth is likely to be associated with both the manufacturing sector (the traditional process) and dynamism in a range of marketed services.[9] Although industrial policies have been converging North and South, there remain crucial differences mainly associated with the present limited policy autonomy of the North. External influences include newly emerging patterns of industrial organization and technology and the creation of a global marketplace. Internal influences relate to the design of a suitable island industrial policy response to meet these new challenges.

The second theme concerns geographical and spatial aspects of island policy, mainly associated with the need for a better integration and improvement of physical infrastructure, but also involving regional and sectoral aspects of industrial policy. In the light of new developments in industrial organization, we re-examine earlier debates on concentration versus dispersal, North and South, in the context of the future of the island economy, where inter-firm collaboration, clustering and the quest for agglomeration economies will become vital to any island-wide success in the future.

The third theme relates to human issues: demography, labour market aspects, and human capital (i.e., educational and training levels). Very rapid demographic changes have taken place in the South during the last decade, and it is anticipated that these will be equally dramatic in the North over the next decade. A lower natural rate of population growth will imply slower growth in the labour force, thus reducing upward pressures on unemployment. Increasingly, economic success must be based on a high level of human capital, and here there are difficult problems to be addressed, North and South. Further improvement in the unemployment situation will need to be associated with improved efficiency of operation of the labour market, and the question arises: would this be assisted by evolution in Northern and Southern institutions?

We draw the above three themes together and combine them with the earlier discussion of economic governance, in order to explain the context for future island growth in chapter 6. Clearly, both regions of the island currently face different policy influences and pressures, and, under most of the possible political scenarios, these will need to continue to coexist with, and be overlaid by, any specific framework of North-South policy collaboration that emerges. This is the essential challenge to politicians and policy-makers, as they seek to design mutually agreed economic policy frameworks that are consistent with the aspirations of all people on the island.

We then examine a series of qualitative scenarios of the likely performance of the island economy under a range of different stylized options (separate, coordinated and single-economy development) and a range of different industrial, infrastructural and demographic/labour market assumptions. This material is intended to complement the previous quantified analysis of short- to medium-term issues carried out by consultants KPMG for the Forum (KPMG 1995). However, our qualitative scenarios are different from the usual notion of an economic forecast, which represents a reasonably firm prediction prepared in the light of very specific world economy and domestic policy assumptions. In fact, the degree of indeterminacy in the likely outcome as indicated by our different scenarios is not a small margin surrounding a neutral centre point. Rather, it is potentially a very wide margin both because of the unavoidable uncertainty that surrounds the assumptions we make, and because analysis of long-term growth is at the very frontier of economic research.

Chapter 7 concludes the main part of our report and draws together its two main themes. First, there are lessons that we can learn from the history of our island economies that may lead to greater North-South understanding of why the two regional economies of this island never achieved the same level of performance during the twentieth century that was achieved by many other small European States and regions. Second, we need to develop and articulate reasonable and shared expectations about the potential that exists for a better economic performance in the future, and work towards a greater understanding of the types of North-South economic cooperation that might best help realize that future.

PART I HISTORY LESSONS

2 THE ORIGINS OF THE TWO ECONOMIES: 1750-1960

Our objective in this chapter is to review briefly some important aspects of the pre-1969 history of the island, taking the view that the 1960s represented a watershed in both political and economic terms, North and South. Policy action taken in the late 1950s and early 1960s launched the Southern economy onto a radically different development path from that which was historically determined. In the North, policy-makers were also forced to face up to the fact that the extraordinary economic successes of the north-east region of Ireland during the middle and late nineteenth century provided a poor foundation for running the late twentieth century economy of a region within the UK. In addition, post-war industrial problems in key traditional Northern sectors were further exacerbated by the events of 1969 and their aftermath.

These more recent developments are still in process and hold out many prospects for improving on the weak performance of both regions of the island during the twentieth century. Later we will address the issue of how modifications to present policies might be used to overcome some of the harm that resulted from the economic divide that occurred in the nineteenth century, a divide that was later reflected in the partition of the two Irish regions into separate political jurisdictions after 1920.

We first discuss some crucial events in the evolution of the island economy since the beginning of the industrial revolution in middle to late eighteenth century Britain. Far from being irrelevant to the economic situation today, these events almost certainly tipped the balance of history and, by excluding alternatives, dominated subsequent developments. One such event, the Great Famine, was apocalyptic even by world standards while others, such as the Act of Union or partition, were of more local consequence.

We then focus on three key economic issues that run as themes through all subsequent economic development on the island. These are the abnormal demographics of the island; the economic geography of the island and the emergence of the North-South divide; and the economic relationships between the island and the rest of the world, including Britain. We conclude with a review of the legacy that pre-1960 history has bequeathed to present-day policy-makers, North and South, the investigation of which will be taken up in the next chapter.

2.1 KEY EVENTS

2.1.1 THE ACT OF UNION

Ireland was on the move in the latter half of the eighteenth century. Under a devolved parliament, however imperfect its structures, economic and social advances were being made at a time when the early effects of the industrial revolution in Britain were beginning to spill over into adjoining countries. Whatever else it did, the Act of Union in 1800 fundamentally changed the terms on which Ireland would relate to the global super-power on its doorstep, and ushered in an era of what has been called 'dependency' or 'capitalist colonization'. After the Union, policy-making adjusted to control from London, and there was to be no protection from the full rigours of competition with the hegemonic British economic giant.

To claim, however, that all economic progress stopped after the Union is grossly simplistic, and in recent years, a number of historians have sought to correct the excesses of this ultra-nationalist type of reaction (Johnson and Kennedy 1991; Ó Gráda 1994). Nevertheless, the nationalist interpretation of the economic history of nineteenth and early twentieth century Ireland was politically influential before, during and after the foundation of the Southern State and its attraction endures even today, thought mostly only in a subliminal form.

The classic statement of the nationalist economic thesis was contained in the writings of George O'Brien (1918 and 1921), the central theme of which is the claim that the absence of political autonomy during the eighteenth and nineteenth centuries condemned Ireland to economic stagnation and decline.[1] Johnson and Kennedy (1991) summarize O'Brien's four main arguments as follows:

- Considerable economic benefits had been conferred on Ireland during the brief period of legislative autonomy that occurred between 1782 and 1800, i.e., by 'Grattan's' Parliament;

- The Act of Union was followed by a long period of economic decline which adversely affected the country in the areas of public finance, agriculture and industry, the causes of which can be directly attributed to the provisions of the Act and the absence of any autonomous local legislative power;

- The strong performance of the economy of the north-east region of the island, centred on Belfast, is explicable in terms of conditions of special advantage that applied only to Ulster;

- The system of land tenure was a long-standing source of Irish economic weakness, but once again Ulster was in a privileged position relative to the rest of the country.

The revising historians challenge the factual basis for at least three of the above four claims. The first claim is held to be inconsistent with the fact that while in many regions of Ireland economic indicators did improve during the last two decades of the eighteenth century, they improved even more in the aftermath of the Union and up to the onset of the Great Famine in the mid-1840s. Also, the Irish Parliament opposed protectionism and favoured free trade. Furthermore, many of the economic improvements had their origins in the early and mid-eighteenth century, well before they could be influenced by Irish parliamentary legislation. Indeed, Johnson and Kennedy conclude that:

> Expansion in agriculture and industry in the period 1750-1800 owed little to Irish parliamentary action. The dynamic of growth was supplied by the market, organizational and technological changes associated with the rise of urban, industrial capitalism in Britain. (P. 16.)

Neither is the second claim borne out by closer examination of the facts. The net contribution to be made by the Irish Exchequer to Britain (2/17 of total British expenditure), was considerably less of a burden when imperial expenditures undertaken in Ireland were taken into account. The Act of Union ensured continued access for Irish agricultural goods to the expanding British market. Furthermore, any adverse changes in the composition of trade in agricultural goods (e.g., a shift from processed meat to live exports), were determined by market conditions and improvements in transport infrastructure that were already in train. A sector-by-sector examination of the performance of Irish industry also shows up the weakness of the nationalist case in blaming the Union. Nor does the success of the north-east region appear to have been built on a land tenure system which encouraged the accumulation of capital. Were it not for the advent of the Great Famine, Johnson and Kennedy's conclusion is difficult to fault on economic grounds in the context of the nineteenth century environment:

> Economic conditions for the exercise of autonomy in the first half of the nineteenth century were far less favourable (than in the second half). Being a region of the UK economy was then, perhaps, the optimal arrangement for Ireland. (P. 28.)

2.1.2 THE GREAT FAMINE

The calamity of the Great Famine, the causes of which had been building up for decades, tore asunder the fragile social and economic fabric of the island and in particular exposed the economic weakness of the densely populated western regions. In his examination of the causes of Ireland's poor economic performance in the nineteenth and twentieth centuries, Lars Mjoset places the post-Famine population decline at the centre of a vicious circle, interacting with and exacerbating what he calls a weak 'national system of innovation' (Mjoset, 1992).[2]

By devastating the population through death and emigration, the Famine prevented the emergence of a dynamic home market for local industry. By bearing most heavily on the more agricultural South, it further accentuated separation from the North. By setting in train a tradition of emigration ('exit'), it dampened internal pressures for economic reform and innovation ('voice').[3] Even today the Great Famine remains an event which, above all others, we in the South use to define ourselves, to explain our problems and to excuse our failures.

The main legacy of the Famine was a gross distortion of the evolution of Ireland's population after the middle of the nineteenth century and creation of the conditions for a very uneven spread of the second Industrial Revolution to Ireland during the second half of that century. Ó Gráda has commented that: 'No other nineteenth century European society endured such an ecological jolt' (Ó Gráda 1994, 235), and concludes that:

The Great Irish Famine is a grim reminder of how narrowly the benefits of the first Industrial Revolution had been spread by the 1840s. Nearly a half century of political and economic union had made little or no impression on the huge gap between Irish and British incomes, nor was it enough to shield Ireland from cataclysm. (P. 208.)

2.1.3 PARTITION

There were strong elements of an economic rationale, seen from Belfast, for partition in the first two decades of this century, at a time when the economy of the north-east of Ireland, centred on that city, was at its zenith. A subsequent irony was that the strong and successful Northern industries — mainly linen, shipbuilding and associated heavy engineering — that required insider access to the British market, were ones that suffered seriously in the aftermath of partition, except for a revival during the abnormal circumstances of the second world war.

Partition was irrelevant to the long-term decline of these Northern sectors, since their pattern of decline was simply mirroring a wider British phenomenon. However, had the non-economic forces leading to partition not been so strong, economic issues might have come more to the fore during the political negotiations of 1920-21. For example, how much did the key Northern industries depend on British orders placed for non-market reasons? How might the inclusion of the industrial North-East in a non-partitioned Ireland have moderated the tensions that led to the economic war of the 1930s, whose most serious consequences affected the South's agricultural sector and pushed the South down a path of protectionist self-sufficiency?

The sundering of the engineering/industrial North from the agricultural/food processing South destroyed any possibility, if there were such, of building intra-island synergies. The centrifugal bonds of identity, tradition and allegiance were simply too strong for the centripetal forces of economic rationality. After partition, North-South trade diminished, sources of supply adjusted, and economic planning on the island accommodated to partition, even if political rhetoric did not.

The view has been often expressed that the partition of Ireland was an economic as well as a political disaster. For example, Mjoset suggests that the loss of Belfast was a once-off event that exacerbated a post-colonial economic vicious circle, since the South was separated from the only surviving industrial centre on the island (Mjoset 1992, 10). However, the dramatic post first world war reversal in the fortunes of the North's two main industries (linen and shipbuilding) raises questions about how much they would have provided innovation and resources for the industrialization which the mainly agricultural South urgently needed.

For example, the 1924 census of production showed that almost 52 per cent of the North's manufacturing labour force was employed in linen, at a time when across the world the demand for linen was in terminal decline (Bardon 1992, 517). Difficulties in Northern shipbuilding were caused by its almost exclusive dependence on a shrinking UK market, at a time when Britain had lost her commercial pre-eminence. It is almost certain that the South's urgent need to construct its industrial sector from an almost zero base, at a time when the world was moving from *laissez faire* to protectionism, would have caused serious North-South policy disputes in any thirty two-county Ireland.[4]

2.2 KEY ECONOMIC ISSUES

Another way to explore the history of Irish development is in terms of key economic issues. Sometimes these can be closely related to a single historical event. For example, the Famine dominates all other explanations in a quest to understand the unique pattern of Irish demographics. However, other issues are associated with a series of events, no one of which is dominant, but which combine and interact to produce a specific economic out-turn.

In this section we identify three such issues, starting with a brief review of demographics. The second key issue concerns the emergence of a North-South divide in the economy, which came eventually to dominate the East-West divide of greater antiquity. The third key issue concerns the manner in which the Irish economy, and later the economies of North and South, came to be almost totally dominated by interactions with Britain, the difficulty in breaking free from this embrace, and the consequences of the British link for policy-making on the island.

2.2.1 DEMOGRAPHICS, EMIGRATION AND DECLINE

Two unique features of Irish demographics stand out clearly. The first, concerning population growth, is illustrated in Figure 2.1, where a comparison is made with a range of other smaller European nations (data from Mjoset 1992). Of the ten comparison countries used by Mjoset, only Ireland showed a decline in population between 1840 and 1910.

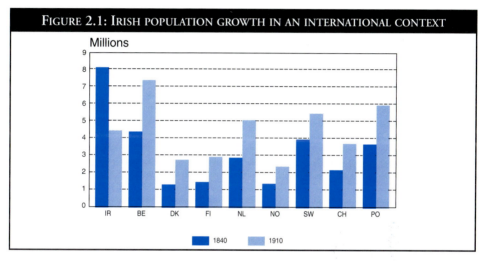

FIGURE 2.1: IRISH POPULATION GROWTH IN AN INTERNATIONAL CONTEXT

The second concerns the extent of Irish migration, where Figure 2.2 makes a comparison with a subset of the three other nations that displayed non-trivial migration behaviour sometime during the period 1851-1960: Denmark, Norway and Sweden. Only for a short period towards the end of the nineteenth century did emigration rates (i.e., emigration per thousand of the population) come anywhere near the high Irish rates.

However, there can be no simple cause and effect explanation of Ireland's poor economic performance, particularly in the twentieth century, in terms of emigration, since emigration could be both a cause of slow growth and an effect of slow growth originating from other failures in the economy. Causes and effects become circular, and the real challenge is to include emigration in a broader study of the Irish pattern of development.

Mjoset's investigations use the notion of a vicious circle linking two key Irish characteristics: population decline via emigration, and a weak national system of innovation (Mjoset 1992, 50-67). These two mechanisms reinforce each other negatively through the social structure: the pastoral bias of agrarian modernization, paternalistic family structures, sluggish growth of the home market, and a further marginalization through weak industrialization. Many of the elements in the weak national system of innovation arise in the context of the economic geography of nineteenth century Ireland, to which we now turn.

2.2.2 ECONOMIC GEOGRAPHY AND THE NORTH-SOUTH DIVIDE

A striking feature of the geography of economic activity is that it often occurs in forms that are highly concentrated spatially. The reasons behind the tendency towards concentration are associated with the presence of increasing returns to scale and agglomeration economies that come from the more intense economic interactions that proximity encourages. For example, the bulk of US manufacturing

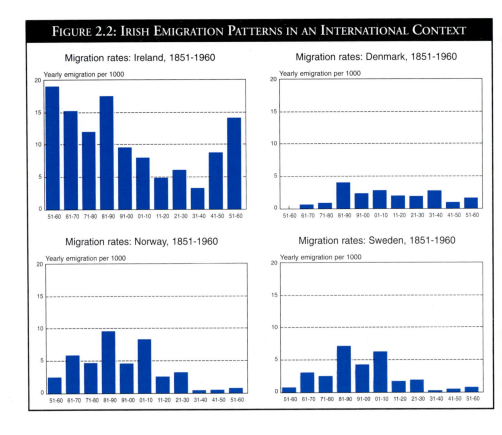

FIGURE 2.2: IRISH EMIGRATION PATTERNS IN AN INTERNATIONAL CONTEXT

industry became concentrated during the second half of the nineteenth century in a relatively small part of the north-east and the eastern part of the mid-west of the US. The resulting manufacturing belt persisted into the second half of the twentieth century, and still contains some 60 per cent of manufacturing employment, down from its 74 per cent share at the turn of the century (Krugman 1991).

Continental Europe has a manufacturing triangle containing the Ruhr, Northern France, and Belgium. Within Britain, the first stage of the Industrial Revolution concentrated in specific areas: Lancashire for cotton, Glasgow (the Clydeside) and Liverpool for shipbuilding, Birmingham for engineering and manufacturing. Hence, it was not entirely surprising that when the Industrial Revolution came to Ireland in the latter half of the nineteenth century, it developed in a geographically concentrated form. However, Ireland's industrialization was never to emulate Britain's generalized economic and technological leap forward. Rather, it was to involve a few specific sectors (brewing, linen, shipbuilding), and selected locations (mainly Dublin and Belfast), and bypassed much of the rest of the country. What is of interest is that the concentration of the key sectors, linen and shipbuilding, came to be located almost exclusively in the north-east corner of the island.

Ó Gráda points out that the common perception of early nineteenth century Ireland as an agricultural economy does not square with the 1821 census that indicated over two-fifths of the population were in occupations such as trades, manufactures, or handicrafts (Ó Gráda 1994, 273). The provincial percentages of the population engaged in such activities ranged from a high of 55 in Ulster to a low of 24 in Munster, with much higher percentages in subregions in the north-east of Ulster (e.g., over 75 per cent in County Armagh). However, little if any of this type of 'proto-industry' had the characteristics of the explosive growth that were typical of the first Industrial Revolution in Britain.[5]

The fortunes of key sectors such as cotton, linen, wool, shipbuilding, and distilling during the first half of the nineteenth century have been documented by Ó Gráda (1994, 273-313). Factors influencing the success or failure of these sectors included access to energy resources (mostly imported coal), the role of entrepreneurship (where the importation of techniques, finance capital, capital goods and skilled workmen played a crucial role, North and South),[6] the possible deterrent role played by crime and civil unrest (which was not reflected, however, in insurance premia relative to Britain), and the price of labour (where lower Irish wages were offset by lower productivity).

Recent advances in the theory of economic growth provide compelling insights into why the Belfast region developed rapidly as the only region in Ireland that fully participated in the latter phases of the Industrial Revolution. In fact, the greater Belfast region took on all the attributes of what economists refer to as an 'industrial district', i.e., a geographically defined productive system characterized by a large number of firms that are involved at various stages and in various ways, in the production of relatively homogeneous products.

A full exploration of the reasons behind the rise of the north-east region would be a major task by itself, and we can merely touch on some of the main factors. For example, events such as the restriction on cotton imports during the American Civil War provided a major boost to the expansion of the factory-based linen industry.[7] However, it was the rise of shipbuilding and engineering, activities that were characterized by much higher wages than the linen mills, which launched Belfast on its path of spectacular growth.

As Bardon points out, chance played a part in ensuring that Edward Harland remained in Belfast, having failed in his initial attempts to attract finance and set up on his own account in Liverpool. Belfast had few of the assets needed to become a great shipbuilding centre, and no notable advantages over other sites in the South. But the actions of the Belfast Harbour Board made the most of it by excavating the Victoria Channel and creating ample space at Queen's Island for future expansion of the shipyards.

Once the shipyards began to grow and become successful, they interacted with local textile industries in creating demand for a huge range in intermediate inputs, such as ropes and rigging, woodwork, metal products, steam engine design and construction, etc. Linen mills created backward linkages to engineering since the construction of steam engines for use in such mills involved boiler-making, and these skills were important in the building of iron ships. Many other examples of user/producer interaction abounded in the greater Belfast region.

Once this process got under way, it became a virtuous circle of cumulative causation, bringing increased economic benefits to the north-east region of Ireland. By the early

1910s two Belfast shipbuilders, Harland & Wolff and Workman Clark, produced over 150,000 tons between them each year, and accounted for 8 per cent of world output and about one quarter of UK tonnage. Indeed, Harland & Wolff had become the biggest shipyard in the world, launching the world's largest ships, while Ulster was the greatest centre of linen production in the world (Ó Gráda 1994, 282-292, and 295-297; Bardon 1992, 306-384). Most strikingly, a decline in population of almost 55 per cent occurred during the years 1841 and 1951 in the area that was eventually to become the Republic of Ireland, compared with a decline of only 17 per cent in the area that was to become Northern Ireland (Mjoset 1992, 222). Population actually grew in the area around Belfast, to the extent that by 1911 the population of the Belfast area (at 386,947) had greatly outstripped that of Dublin (at 304,802).

2.2.3 Relations with the Rest of the World

The political incorporation of Ireland into the UK in 1801 generated forces that led to a comprehensive economic and trade integration as well. The full extent of this integration after more than 100 years of Union is illustrated in Figure 2.3 for the case of the South. This figure shows the UK-Irish trade position from just after partition to 1950. The proportion of Southern exports going to the UK showed a very small reduction from 98.6 per cent in 1924 to 92.7 per cent by 1950. The decline in imports was more marked: 81.1 per cent originated in the UK in 1924, and this had fallen to 52.9 by the year 1950.

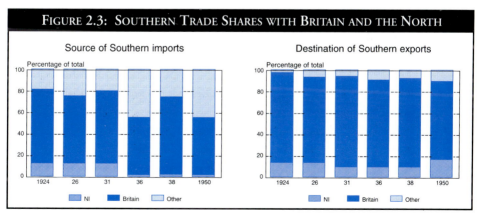

FIGURE 2.3: SOUTHERN TRADE SHARES WITH BRITAIN AND THE NORTH

The failure of the South to diversify its economy away from an almost total dependence on the UK had serious consequences for its economic performance. The poor performance of the Southern economy when compared with a range of other small European countries has been the subject of much research and comment.[8] The reluctance of the new Southern public administration to deviate too much from British policy norms has been well documented (Fanning 1978). The inability of the new Northern administration to deviate in any significant way at all from UK-wide policy decisions simply reflected the extremely limited scope for local autonomy that was provided for in the 1920 Government of Ireland Act.

Starting from a position of almost full economic integration within the UK, it is hard not to be sympathetic with Southern policy-makers as they considered their options. The eventual break with *laissez faire* that came with the first change of administration in 1932 was not, in fact, such a dramatic step, since protection had been creeping into the international economy during the 1920s and the world financial system that had supported free trade was being rocked to its foundations.[9]

The nature of the difficulties faced by the South in breaking free from the economic embrace of the UK are well illustrated by the behaviour of trade within the EC over the past thirty to forty years. Thomsen and Woolcock, 1993 point out that the exports from individual countries to the rest of Europe are still highly concentrated in only a few markets. For example, the top three export markets within the Union for each member State take in between 56 and 77 per cent of total intra-EU exports from that country, with the largest economies figuring prominently in this list (Germany, France, the UK), but export market proximity as well as size is a factor. Market size, distance, common borders and similar languages strongly influence intra-industry trade and the pattern of overall trade in Europe.

This has led Wijkman (1990) to extend the analysis of geographical factors by looking at what he calls 'webs of dependency'. He suggests that there are three sub-regional trade blocs in Europe. The first is the *North* periphery, consisting of the UK, the Republic of Ireland, and Scandinavia. The second is the *South* periphery, comprising the Iberian peninsula, Greece and Turkey. The remaining countries are clustered around Germany and called *Core Europe*. Comparing the trade pattern of 1958 with that in 1987, Wijkman found that in many cases these clusters have become more, rather than less, clearly defined as a result of greater EU integration. However, we shall see that the (Southern) Irish relationship with Britain, which had been among the very strongest webs of dependency prior to 1960, weakened considerably thereafter for very specific reasons.

It was hardly surprising that these islands formed a particularly strong web of dependency, continuing from independence well into the 1960s. While Southern Irish policies and policy-makers may have been less assertive and innovative than might have been desired, in the absence of a robust industrial sector there is probably very little that could have been achieved to accelerate an earlier economic decoupling of the South from the UK. The consequences for the South followed inexorably. In the words of Mjoset (1992):

> Ireland became a free rider on Britain's decline, while Austria and Switzerland were free riders on Germany's economic miracle. Even Belfast specialized in lines of production which fitted into the general British orientation: textiles and shipbuilding. (P. 9.)

The strong web of dependency between the South and the UK began to weaken only after the shift to foreign direct investment and export-led growth that followed the various programmes for economic expansion in the late 1950s and during the 1960s. Figure 2.4 shows the behaviour of the shares of Southern exports going to the UK, and Southern imports originating in the UK, for the period 1960-92. The forces that brought about this changed pattern of behaviour are further explored in the next chapter.

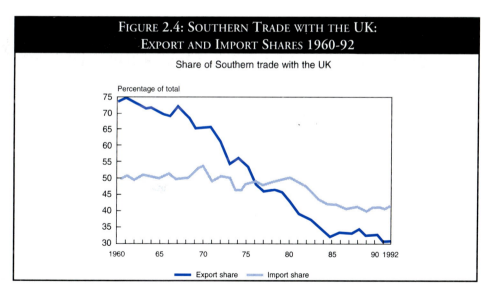

FIGURE 2.4: SOUTHERN TRADE WITH THE UK: EXPORT AND IMPORT SHARES 1960-92

Share of Southern trade with the UK

Even after a period of thirty years exposure to foreign direct investment, however, the same essential dilemma exists for the South and the North, and has been summarized in slightly more political terms:

Governments in small, open economies are severely limited in what they can achieve in terms of industrial development, more especially when they function essentially as client economies. The Republic has become increasingly a client state of international business. While this is also true of the North, this spatial unit has the added problem of being a client region of a state experiencing significant industrial decline. (Brunt 1989, 229-230)

2.3 LEGACY: THE TWO ECONOMIES IN THE 1960s

The South embarked on a path of political independence with an economy that was without significant industrialization, but was dependent on mainly agricultural exports to the British market. The North achieved regional autonomy within the UK at a stage when the perilous state of its strong industrial base was still hidden in the aftermath of the economic boom created by the first world war. The relative positions of North and South are illustrated in Figure 2.5, which shows the approximate Northern 'share' of gross industrial output just before 1914. Other than the range of food processing activities, such as grain milling, brewing and malting, butter, cheese, bacon curing, etc., the South was virtually without industries at this time, while the North's success was built on linen, engineering, and shipbuilding (Ó Gráda 1994, 312-313).

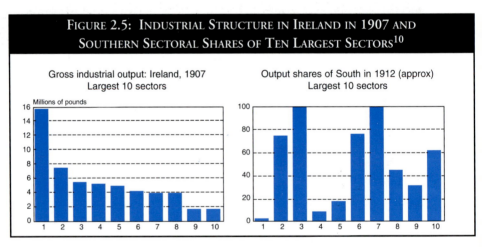

FIGURE 2.5: INDUSTRIAL STRUCTURE IN IRELAND IN 1907 AND SOUTHERN SECTORAL SHARES OF TEN LARGEST SECTORS[10]

Between 1922 and the early 1960s there were many changes in the North and South, but few of major significance compared with the legacy of the pre-1922 period. The South constructed an industrial base behind a protective barrier of high tariffs. The North's staple industrial specializations continued in decline, with a temporary interruption during the second world war. Both regions entered the 1960s in a state where major policy changes were needed, even in a situation where the North had been moderately successful during the 1950s in attracting British investment in the area of textiles, artificial fibres and other petroleum-based products. What was not anticipated was that the outbreak of the troubles would make this transformation much more prolonged and difficult than it would have been in a period of peaceful economic transition.

Some important lessons can be learned from the economic history of the island over the last century and a half. First, the modern features of the island economy were clearly present from the middle of the nineteenth century. These included a weak island industrial base, other than in the north-east corner of the island; the interaction of population growth with weak economic performance that was to appear as a mixture of unemployment/under-employment and emigration; a vicious circle of interaction between emigration and a weak ability to create a national system of innovation; and an almost complete integration into and dependence on the British economy.

Only after a period of national crisis was a sustained effort made in the South to address these problems with the publication of *Economic Development* and *The First Programme for Economic Expansion* in 1958 (Stationery Office 1958). Parallel efforts were made in the North during the 1950s and 1960s and produced a rate of Northern industrial-based growth that exceeded that of Britain (Farley 1995). However, subsequent efforts were hampered by the OPEC I oil price crisis and the slow-down in world growth, by a lack of appropriate regional policy instruments and by the effects of the outbreak and persistence of the troubles from the late 1960s.

The fragmentation of the island economy, that had roots in the extraordinary late nineteenth century success of the north-east region, has little enduring logic in the last decade of the twentieth century. The challenge to policy-makers today will be to design political solutions that might permit long-suppressed natural benefits of the island economy to emerge, while also meeting other, more political requirements. These issues are taken up in later chapters.

3 THE TWO ECONOMIES DURING THE TROUBLES: 1960-94

Having scanned two centuries of economic history, we now narrow our focus to the three most recent decades, examining the twenty five years since the escalation of the troubles in the North in the late 1960s. The damage done to the North, and to a lesser extent to the South, is only now beginning to be understood and addressed.

Although economists of nationalist and unionist hues are likely to interpret the socio-economic record of recent decades with differing degrees of emphasis, the facts tend to speak for themselves.[1] However, the ESRI and NIERC medium-term studies of the two regions are examples of analyses that have tended to ignore North-South inter-comparisons and island economy issues.[2] In part this simply reflects perceptions of the very limited economic interactions between the two regions and the restricted way in which the prospects for future beneficial interactions are considered by practising forecasters.

At the other extreme are economic analyses of 'new' types of Ireland. For example, Dowling, (1974) examined the economics of a unified Ireland and a recent updated recalculation along the same lines has been provided by the Cadogan Group (Cadogan Group 1992). The New Ireland Forum studied some of the macroeconomic and public finance consequences of three possible alternative political arrangements on the island: a unitary State, a federal or confederal State, and joint authority (Stationery Office 1984). O'Leary et al. (1993) updates these types of calculations for a shared authority model of governance. However, this type of ex ante quantitative politico-economic cost-benefit analysis needs to make very strong theoretical and practical assumptions and must be undertaken with great care. For example, the implicit political and institutional assumptions that motivate such studies would be likely to induce so much change in the underlying economic performance of the private sectors, North and South, as to call into question the relevance of any analysis that focused mainly on public sector fiscal matters.

In reading the extensive economic literatures of the Northern and Southern economies one is constantly being reminded of the very different mind sets of the North and the South. For example, in a recent NIEC report (1991) examining the broad policy options for the North — a document of remarkable frankness and insight — the following sentence occurs: 'By virtue of its physical separation from the rest of the UK and position in relation to Europe, Northern Ireland cannot be said to have any strategic advantage in location.' (P. 4.) The economic literature of the South is littered with similar references to its own peripheral situation. Hence, one cannot avoid the conclusion that in the past each region saw its peripherality not in the context of the island of Ireland, encompassing — in an entirely benign way — the similar plight of the other region, but in a more exclusive way that placed little value on the market potential of the other region or of the island economy as a whole.[3]

Of more immediate practical use are attempts to describe the two regions in the context of their existing, unchanged political and institutional arrangements. Even without invoking major institutional changes, this is a difficult enough task by itself, and one that has not been carried out in an entirely satisfactory way, North or South. The goal of such descriptions should be the identification of actual or potential bottlenecks to better economic performance in the two regions. If such an examination leads one to conclude that particular economic failures can be credibly attributed to inappropriate and restrictive political and institutional arrangements, and if such an attribution were acceptable to people in the North and the South, then a rational economic basis for political dialogue between the two regions might be established.

Despite the difference in political status of the economies of North and South, both share an extensive dependence on the external world. The external trade links of the North are dominated by sales to British markets and the external multinational presence in the North has been dominated by British firms. Prior to 1960 the South's trading and other external links were similarly British oriented, but since then the sources of imports and the destination of exports have diversified considerably.

Furthermore, the US rather than Britain has played the leading role in inward foreign direct investment in the South. The importance of the British-Irish influence works the other way as well. For example, the South is the UK's fifth most important export destination, taking an export share of 5.1 per cent, nearly half of the 12.7 per cent share of Germany — the largest single destination — and is the only major trading partner with which the UK runs a trade surplus, amounting to about £1 billion in 1990.

In addition to world trade and multinational investment flows, there are large migrant labour movements specifically between the island of Ireland and Britain which are crucial to an understanding of the island's two economies. The openness of the labour markets on the island of Ireland means that the migration mechanism plays a major role in adjusting regional labour supply and demand, and heavily influences regional wage setting, particularly in the South, in a way that is unique among developed economies.[4]

Their close geographical proximity and common land border, the strength of their external linkages, and the degree of economic dependence on Britain that these imply, make it useful, despite their difference in political status, to study the Northern and Southern economies in a common framework both as regions within the grouping of these two islands and within the wider European Union. In addition, the two Irish regions have many economic and social problems in common: serious long-term unemployment; demographic trends that are at variance with other EU States; a generally poor competitiveness and innovation performance of indigenous industry;[5] extreme vulnerability to external economic influences (world growth, in the case of the South, and British fiscal policy in the case of the North), over-dependency on external and foreign multinationals; imbalances in the public finances that were explicit in the South and implicit in the North.

Although North and South share many economic characteristics and problems, the published literature contains virtually no attempts to place analysis within a common regional economic framework.[6] Rather, the North is usually discussed in the context of the eleven sub-regions of the UK (Harris 1991) and the South in the context of a small peripheral member State of the EU (Bradley et al. 1995).[7] To an outsider it might seem the most natural and interesting thing in the world to compare the economies of North and South. Making allowance for their different economic structures at the time of the partition of the island in 1921, such a comparison can fruitfully address the fascinating question of the extent to which political and economic institutions, culture, attitudes to enterprise and innovation, and personal characteristics condition economic performance (Mjoset 1992). Nevertheless, there are few descriptions of both regions that start off from an assumption that their structure, and the forces that drive them, have more similarities than differences. We have seen above that what one does find are, at the one extreme, descriptions of both regions in isolation from each other and, at the other extreme, attempts to portray how the two regions might perform under radically changed political arrangements.

Given their shared regional and peripheral characteristics, many interesting issues can be addressed within a comparative study of the two economies of Ireland. For example:

- From having been the most heavily industrialized region of the island of Ireland, the North has seen its manufacturing sector decline sharply since the 1960s and, at least relative to the more dynamic behaviour of the South, it has failed to capture adequate substitute multinational investment. What are the consequences of this relative decline and difference in performance?

- The North is now in receipt of large-scale regional transfers within the UK. What effects have these transfers had on the structure of the Northern economy compared with the effect of the parallel extensive public sector borrowing on the economic performance of the South?

- Given the difference in structure and behaviour of the Northern and Southern economies, how does each separate region react to shocks in external or world factors?

- More generally, what is the potential for accelerated growth and development in the North and the South, an acceleration that will be needed if the relative position of both regions towards the lower end of the EU league table is to be improved?

In this chapter we provide an overview of the economies of both regions for the period of the troubles, focusing on six key issues:
1. The behaviour of the private sector (mainly manufacturing, but including

market services), which must be the ultimate engine of regional growth.

2. The role played by the public sector, in offsetting the costs of the troubles in the North and in improving the level of public services of all kinds in the South.

3. The behaviour of the two labour markets, as unemployment soared in both regions during the 1980s.

4. Issues that arose in paying for public sector activity such as public employment, investment and income transfers.

5. Regional competitiveness and the trade balance.

6. Methods used to quantify the costs of the troubles to the North, and the more modest knock-on costs to the South.

3.1 THE PRIVATE SECTOR

3.1.1 MANUFACTURING

The manufacturing sector of a modern small open regional economy is very directly exposed to competition in the wider external or international marketplace. We saw in chapter 2 that for the earlier period 1932-1960 there had been rapid growth of all kinds of indigenous industry in the South, protected from international competition by high tariff barriers. However, after the advent of the Anglo-Irish Free Trade Agreement in 1965 and EC entry in 1973, much of this industrial base vanished, unable to compete with more efficient foreign firms (Kennedy, Giblin and McHugh 1988). Northern Ireland, of course, always functioned in a regime of free trade, with full access to the large British and Commonwealth markets.

Since both regional Irish home markets were so small, the domestic traded sectors, North and South, simply could not efficiently supply all their different needs through import substitution. Rather, they needed to specialize in a narrow range of products, sell in highly competitive export markets, and import the goods not produced at home. As they moved to such specialization, the two most striking aspects of manufacturing activity on the island over the last three decades are that total employment has remained almost unchanged (359,000 in 1960 compared with 343,000 in 1990), while a dramatic shift in favour of the South was taking place (Figure 3.1).

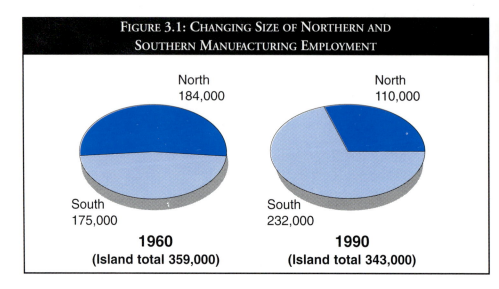

FIGURE 3.1: CHANGING SIZE OF NORTHERN AND SOUTHERN MANUFACTURING EMPLOYMENT

North
184,000

North
110,000

South
175,000

South
232,000

1960
(Island total 359,000)

1990
(Island total 343,000)

The evolution since the 1960s of aggregate Northern and Southern manufacturing employment is shown in Figure 3.2. While Northern manufacturing output (more accurately, GDP arising in the manufacturing sector) stagnated, Southern manufacturing output rose rapidly, even adjusting for distortion of the figures due to transfer pricing by foreign multinationals and the associated profit repatriation.[8] Also, in contrast to relatively buoyant Southern manufacturing investment, driven largely by foreign direct investment, Northern manufacturing investment largely stagnated during the troubles.

The stagnation of Northern manufacturing was accompanied by a massive shedding of labour and had serious consequences for the wider Northern economy. However, despite the strong growth in output, the performance of Southern manufacturing employment was disappointing. The decline of labour intensive traditional industries was accompanied by rapid growth in high technology capital and R&D intensive domestic firms and foreign multinationals. The result of these two offsetting patterns was that total Southern manufacturing employment grew to a peak in 1980 of

250,000, but declined during the prolonged post OPEC II recession to just under 230,000 in 1994.

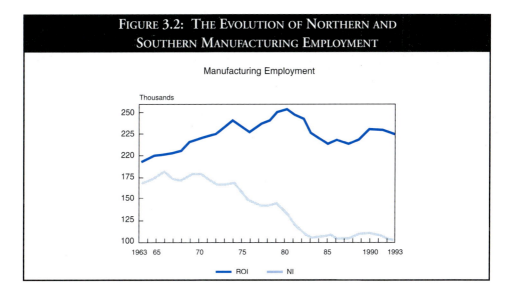

FIGURE 3.2: THE EVOLUTION OF NORTHERN AND SOUTHERN MANUFACTURING EMPLOYMENT

The decline of the Northern manufacturing sector relative to the South and, in particular, the decline of Northern manufacturing employment in absolute terms, are key Irish economic events of the last three decades for which we need explanations. There are two very obvious questions that arise from this contrast in manufacturing behaviour. First, was the North-South difference in manufacturing performance due mainly to the civil unrest in the North, starting in the late 1960s and continuing to late 1994? Second, was it due to a greater policy flexibility enjoyed by the South, with the South's ability to deviate, to some extent, from UK policy norms?

Concerning the troubles factor and Northern industrial decline, there is a certain amount of research on the quantification of the economic effects of civil unrest, but no very convincing conclusions. In such research, all Northern under-performance relative to other UK regions tends to be attributed purely to the troubles (see section 3.6 below). However, the troubles factor, no matter how serious and substantial, is inextricably linked to the role played by public expenditure in attempting to mitigate the negative consequences of the civil unrest. This role involved such policies as capital and labour subsidies, increased public sector employment, public sector purchases of goods and services, improved infrastructure, education and training expenditures, etc. In the absence of this public financial support, the decline of the indigenous Northern manufacturing sector, together with the wider non-manufacturing economy, would undoubtedly have been much worse.[9]

On the other hand, the inability of the North to attract inward investment to anything like the extent of the South can probably be blamed partially on the uncertainty and disruption of the troubles as well as on world economic conditions. However, the fact that the troubles coincided with a serious crisis in Northern industrial policy suggests that it is useless to attempt to pin the subsequent decline on the troubles per se (Munck 1993, 60-64).

Concerning the second (policy flexibility) factor, comparison of Northern employment performance with aggregate UK performance shows that Northern Ireland was merely tracking a wider UK manufacturing decline, as Figure 3.3 illustrates, without the parallel strong growth of private services that occurred in the more prosperous core British regions in the South and Midlands. The North, together with other relatively poorer peripheral British regions, appears to have been unable to arrest this decline with the limited range of policy instruments and the level of support available (NIEC 1992, 21). Specific Northern Ireland comparisons with Scotland tend to reinforce this finding (NIEC 1992, 38-43). It seems reasonable to suggest that the Northern decline relative to the South was due at least in part to a lack of policy flexibility in the North rather than to poor implementation of available Northern policies.

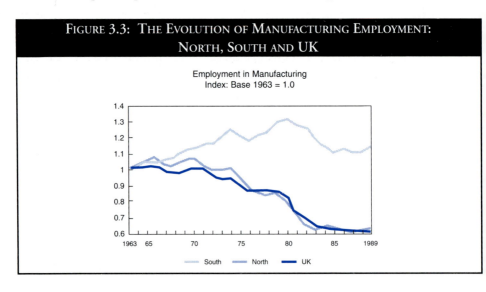

FIGURE 3.3: THE EVOLUTION OF MANUFACTURING EMPLOYMENT: NORTH, SOUTH AND UK

The performance of the Southern manufacturing sector may look flattering in comparison with the North, but contains a disturbing difference between the inability of the Southern indigenous sector to grow and compete internationally, and a more rapid growth of the less employment-intensive foreign-owned sector (NESC 1992). In Figure 3.4 we illustrate the different employment performances of three sub-sectors of Southern manufacturing: high technology (largely foreign-owned), food processing, and other traditional (mainly indigenous) manufacturing. The data show the dramatic rise in importance of the largely foreign-owned high technology sector relative to the traditional sector.

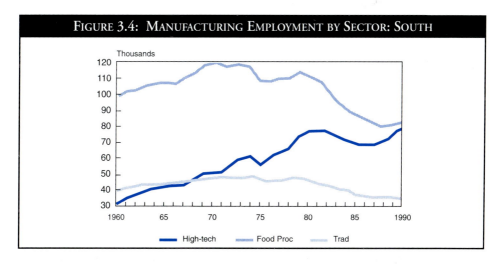

FIGURE 3.4: MANUFACTURING EMPLOYMENT BY SECTOR: SOUTH

As Teague (1987) has observed, the relative stagnation of the Northern and Southern economies during the 1950s led policy-makers in both regions simultaneously to make fundamental re-evaluations of industrial policy and actively seek foreign direct investment. Both regions designed attractive investment grants and factory building schemes. In the South, a zero rate of tax on profits arising from exports was put in place in the late 1950s, replaced after EC entry in 1973 by a flat rate of 10 per cent on profits in manufacturing. In the British policy as applied in the North, a regional employment premium (REP) scheme of wage subsidies was included, among other subsidy- and grant-based policies.

Foreign investment in both regions grew rapidly over the period 1958 to 1975, mainly in the engineering and textiles sectors. The South has continued to benefit from a continuing inflow of foreign investment, interrupted only temporarily by the

OPEC I and II world recessions, and continuing thereafter at a somewhat slower rate, reflecting slower world growth. In the South, the emphasis in foreign direct investment shifted to computer, chemical and pharmaceutical products in the 1970s and 1980s. However, many of the earlier Northern multinational projects were lost (particularly in the artificial fibre sector) and the ability of the North to attract new replacement multinational investment in high technology areas was considerably weaker than that in the South (NIEC 1992).

The earlier high level of Northern industrialization relative to the more agricultural South was significant in two respects, as a visible sign of economic superiority and increasing the likelihood of Northern self-sufficiency within the UK. Even as late as 1960 there were still more people employed in manufacturing in the North than in the South, in spite of the latter's larger population base. During the 1970s and early 1980s this position changed dramatically, for a variety of reasons: the decline of older 'sunset' industries in the UK and elsewhere; wider economic problems in the slow-growing UK economy, the consequences of which were exacerbated by the continuing very close links between the North and Britain; restricted scope for regional fiscal and development policies compared with the more autonomous South; and the inability of the North to win a sizeable share of US direct investment.

The Southern story was very different. After tariff barriers were dismantled in the 1960s, there was a shake-out of inefficient indigenous firms that were unable to adjust to world competition, and whose survival had depended on protection. Within the indigenous sector, the progressive rationalization of food processing through mergers and take-overs led to improved scale efficiencies and increased exports. Finally, the South captured a large share of internationally mobile — mainly US — high technology investment, attracted by generous financial incentives and the high level of human capital.

Whatever modest dynamism the Southern economy has probably stems from the better performance of its manufacturing sector relative to that of the North. This includes a greater Southern ability to attract inward multinational investment, the orientation of industry towards products that have high income elasticities (such as computers and pharmaceuticals), and a greater openness to EU markets other than Britain.[10] The failure of the North to secure a strong flow of non-British inward foreign direct investment in the most recent decades is a key distinguishing feature in any comparison with the South.

3.1.2 MARKET SERVICES

The main components of the market services sector are transport, communications, distribution, finance, insurance and other personal and business services. Another category of services consists of building and construction and utilities (electricity, gas and water). To a large extent these activities are directed at the domestic market, although elements of financial and construction services are becoming increasingly traded on international markets.[11]

The relationship of the market services sector with the manufacturing sector has been changing over the years as many activities previously carried out in the manufacturing sector are being transferred to the service sector. In Figure 3.5 we show the evolution of employment in the market services sector, North and South. In both cases the sector has grown, in stark contrast to the manufacturing sector for Northern Ireland shown in Figure 3.2 above. However, the service sector growth in the South may have had more to do with the provision of services to the increasingly complex manufacturing sector than in the North, where it may be more associated with the phenomenal growth of the public sector (see below).[12]

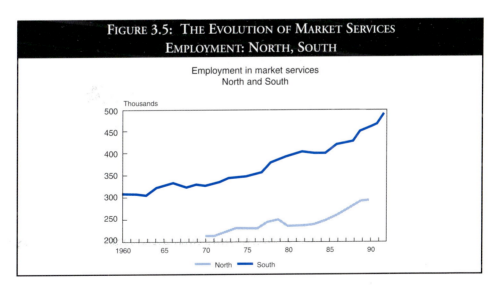

FIGURE 3.5: THE EVOLUTION OF MARKET SERVICES EMPLOYMENT: NORTH, SOUTH

The tourism sector is a particularly important element of market services. Here the effects of the troubles were serious. Southern earnings from tourism in 1967 amounted to £565 million in 1985 prices. Only in 1988 did real earnings exceed this figure. Given the high 'multiplier' associated with tourism earnings, and the regional dispersal of these earnings, the negative economic impact on North and South was very great, but less dramatic than high profile factory closures in terms of publicity.[13]

There is a tendency in economic analysis to treat the market services sector as being derivative and subservient to the more traditionally dynamic manufacturing sector, and this is reflected in our discussion above. However, this situation is likely to change very rapidly over the next few years, mainly due to the extensive deregulation of a wide range of services such as transport, telecommunications, electricity, gas, etc. We return to these issues later in chapter 6.

3.1.3 AGRICULTURE

Employment in the two regional agricultural sectors is shown in Figure 3.6, both in absolute terms (A) and as a percentage of total employment (B). Although the shake-out of labour from Northern agriculture started earlier than in the South, mirroring the even earlier decline of British agricultural employment during and after the Industrial Revolution, both regions display a similar pattern of employment decline, in absolute terms and as a share of total employment. Given the decline of Northern manufacturing referred to above, the Northern employment share in agriculture has tended to stabilize in more recent years.

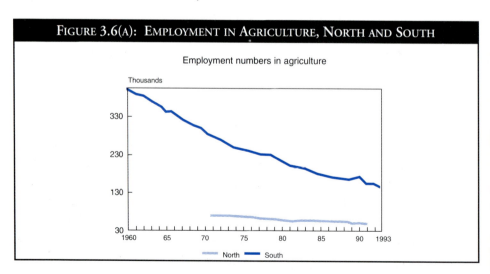

FIGURE 3.6(A): EMPLOYMENT IN AGRICULTURE, NORTH AND SOUTH

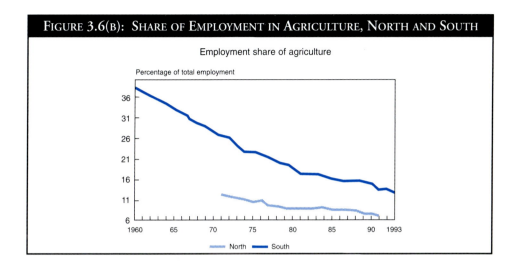

FIGURE 3.6(B): SHARE OF EMPLOYMENT IN AGRICULTURE, NORTH AND SOUTH

3.2 THE PUBLIC SECTOR

Our definition of the public sector is quite wide, embracing public administration, policing, defence, health, education, etc. Basically, all employees in this sector have their salaries and wages paid out of the public purse, i.e. from tax revenue or from borrowing. While employment grew rapidly both North and South, the actual size of the Northern sector is quite phenomenal, compared with the size of the private sector. To illustrate this we show public sector (or non-market sector) employment in Figure 3.7 as a percentage of private (or market) sector employment (i.e., manufacturing, market services and agriculture). In a sense this is the 'burden' carried by a region's private sector to the extent that regional tax revenue supports the public sector.

A special factor driving up the numbers employed in the Northern public sector over the past twenty five years was the need to increase the size of the security forces. The bulk of the increase in the size of the army never appeared in the Northern labour force, being a charge on the UK as a whole. However, the increased numbers employed in the RUC, the Royal Irish Regiment, and the prison service did appear in Northern public sector employment statistics, serving to inflate them greatly relative to the situation that would have prevailed in a period of peace.[14] Total employment in the security area was estimated to be 24,500 in 1995. After a complete transition to peace, and based on British norms, it has been estimated that these numbers could be reduced by as much as 50 per cent, i.e., to 12,700 (KPMG

1995, 44-46). However, most scenarios considered in the KPMG study envisaged a reallocation of expenditure to other areas of the non-security public sector, so it remains problematic if the overall numbers can be easily reduced.

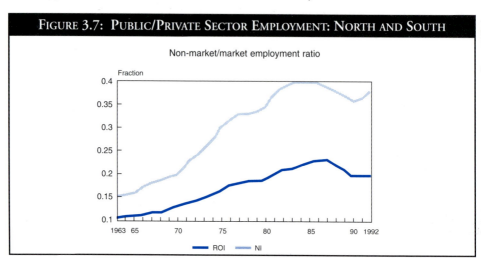

FIGURE 3.7: PUBLIC/PRIVATE SECTOR EMPLOYMENT: NORTH AND SOUTH

Non-market/market employment ratio

What Figure 3.7 illustrates is that the Northern public sector is dramatically larger than its Southern counterpart, relative to the size of the market sector. The relationship between the exposed manufacturing sector (which is forced to match world prices and is driven mainly by external demand) and the non-market sector is a particularly interesting one. In the South, as we shall see below, the need to finance public sector expansion by immediate or deferred taxation (i.e., debt creation) drives a 'wedge' between wage costs borne by employers in manufacturing and the take home wage spent by the worker on consumer goods. Hence, public sector expansion can crowd out employment in the exposed manufacturing sector through loss of competitiveness as unions drive up nominal wages to restore their real standard of living. This tended to happen in the South during the 1980s and was a cause of serious loss of manufacturing jobs (Barry and Bradley 1991).

In the North, on the other hand, there is now no immediate link between the size of the public sector and the need to finance it exclusively from Northern Ireland tax resources. Part of the explanation of the behaviour of the public/private employment ratio can be attributed to the need for the North to catch up with British levels of public services. In addition, the small size of the private sector magnifies the ratio. However, the increase in the size of the public sector can still crowd out the exposed manufacturing sector through the effect of the lower rate of regional unemployment in driving up wage rates (Bradley and Wright 1992). Causation is difficult to establish here: the growth in public sector employment may have been a rational and deliberate policy response by the UK Government to the poor performance of the Northern manufacturing sector. On the other hand, a massive autonomous growth of the public sector may have exacerbated the cost competitiveness problems of Northern manufacturing by driving up wages in the North and absorbing too much of the talented workforce into the provision of high wage public services.

In summary, as the Northern manufacturing sector contracted during the 1970s, much of the slack was taken up by the expansion of the public sector, which had knock-on demand benefits for market services and the smaller, less export oriented manufacturing firms. Decisions taken to provide social and other public services to the North on the basis of 'need' relative to British norms, together with escalating security expenditure, broke the previous pattern of decades of moderate Northern public sector deficits. The North shifted into a situation of chronic structural deficits, amounting today to some 25 per cent of Northern GDP. If Northern policy-makers remain indifferent to the size of these deficits, and regard the subvention as an enduring aspect of their economy, then the North risks becoming trapped in a Mezzogiorno-like problem of permanent dependency.[15]

The situation in the South has some uneasy parallels with the North. Economic growth during the 1960s, proximity to Britain and close familiarity with British standards, and entry into the EEC in the 1970s, brought with it pressure for a bigger public sector role. This pressure culminated in the late 1970s in an explosive growth of public spending, which was followed after the second OPEC world recession, by an unsustainable rise in the public debt. The necessity to tackle the fiscal crisis by a combination of tax increases and expenditure cuts caused the South's recession to be long and deep, but produced the basis for a healthier period of high growth that has lasted to the present day. This period provided salutary lessons for the South that have relevance for the North, in that it illustrates how a small economy can achieve fundamental change, even with a limited range of policy instruments.

For a variety of reasons, the Northern public sector is very much larger, in terms of its share of GDP, than that of the South, with a corresponding higher level and quality of services. A beneficial effect of this for the North is that, given continued finance, the Northern economy is partially shielded from the vicissitudes of the rest of the world. However, a negative effect is that the Northern economy may be less responsive to up-turns in the external economic environment given that the public sector dominates such a large fraction of the regional economy.

3.3 LABOUR MARKET FAILURE

A shared feature of the two labour markets on the island of Ireland has been the enduring high rate of unemployment in both regions. In Figure 3.8 we show both North, South and British unemployment rates.[16] In Figures 3.9(A) and 3.9(B) we show the annual change in the working age population superimposed on net migration to and from each region.

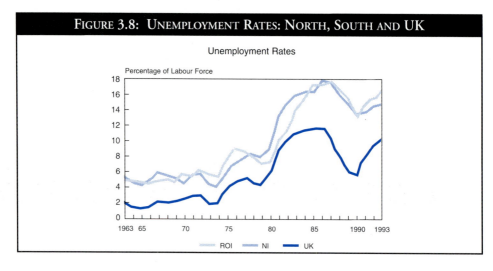

FIGURE 3.8: UNEMPLOYMENT RATES: NORTH, SOUTH AND UK

The common pattern of behaviour of unemployment is striking. During the 1980s, both Irish regions suffered much higher rises in unemployment rates than occurred in Britain. In addition, the gap between unemployment rates in Britain and in the South has risen much more dramatically than has the gap between unemployment rates in Britain and the North (the period of unsustainable fiscal expansion of 1978-81 being a temporary exception). The Northern situation might well have been much more serious if it were not for the increased role of the public sector, described above.

The patterns of labour migration and population growth, however, are very dissimilar in the two Irish regions. In the case of the South, migration was net outward during the 1960s, became strongly net inward during the expansionary

1970s, and reverted to net outward for most of the 1980s. In the last few years net outward migration has essentially ceased, due to the deterioration of the British labour market and the relative improvement in social welfare entitlements in the South.[17] In the case of the North, migration has been more modest and steady, other than during the years 1971-72 which was a period of very serious civil unrest involving a heavy death and injury toll.[18]

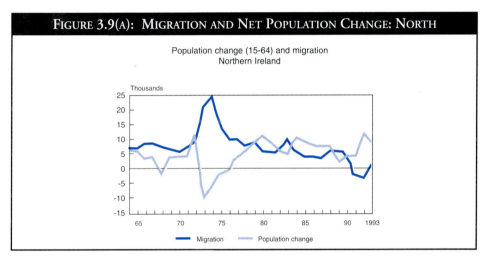

FIGURE 3.9(A): MIGRATION AND NET POPULATION CHANGE: NORTH

Population change (15-64) and migration
Northern Ireland

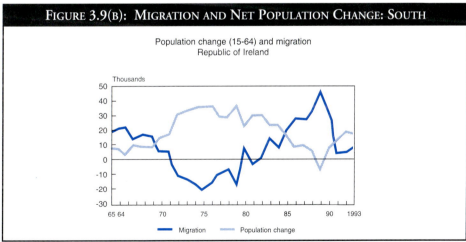

FIGURE 3.9(B): MIGRATION AND NET POPULATION CHANGE: SOUTH

Population change (15-64) and migration
Republic of Ireland

The existence of migration flows, either actual or potential, has important consequences for the operation of the labour market and the determination of regional wage rates. Ireland, North and South, has large pools of potential emigrants at home and potential return migrants overseas. These migration flows are sensitive to regional Irish/British unemployment and wage differentials, although empirically, unemployment differentials appear more important. Expansion of employment in either Irish region is likely, in the long run, to reduce emigration much more than it will reduce unemployment.[19]

In the 1980s, the historical relationship between aggregate Southern and British unemployment rates broke down, but Honohan (1992) has argued that British unemployment rates continue to exercise a dominant role on Southern male unemployment rates in the long run. However, the equilibrium differential appears to be increasing over time. One possible interpretation for this may lie in the fact that unemployment benefit, assistance and other social welfare rates in the South, even if at a lower level than British rates until recently, have risen faster than those in Britain. This is a factor of critical importance in relation to the Southern unemployment problem. Thus, while the unemployment differential does not appear to be beyond the influence of policy-makers, this does indicate the inadequacy of demand-led employment stimuli as a measure for reducing Southern unemployment as distinct from increasing employment.

The situation in the North is quite analogous to that in the South, except that the British social welfare system has applied in the North, including for the duration of the troubles, thus lessening the propensity towards outward migration. Nor has regional policy been any more effective in lowering the Northern unemployment rate than in the South. For example, Roper and O'Shea (1991), based on simulations using the NIMOD model of the North, analysed the effects of the higher than UK average Northern Regional Employment Premium (REP). They suggest that the initial benefits of the REP in boosting employment and reducing unemployment during the early years of its operation were offset later by reduced emigration. In fact they conclude that the long-term legacy of the labour subsidies of the 1970s was to increase the rate of unemployment subsequently in the mid-1980s, after the REP was abolished in 1979.

A further serious characteristic of Northern and Southern labour markets is that the fraction of those who are long-term unemployed (defined as greater than one year) has become very high over the last decade (Figures 3.10(A) and 3.10(B)).

Furthermore, in the North this has been associated with pockets of long-term unemployment in areas that have suffered most from the troubles (Figure 3.11 (A)). The regional variation in unemployment rates was not so pronounced in the South, at least not at the level of regional subdivision shown in the graph.[20]

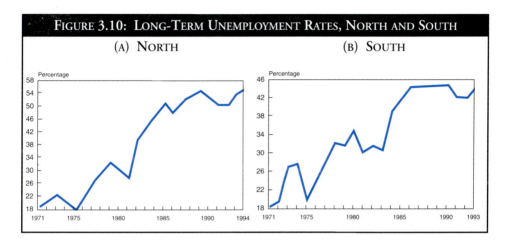

FIGURE 3.10: LONG-TERM UNEMPLOYMENT RATES, NORTH AND SOUTH
(A) NORTH (B) SOUTH

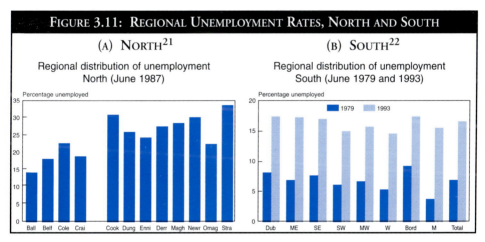

FIGURE 3.11: REGIONAL UNEMPLOYMENT RATES, NORTH AND SOUTH
(A) NORTH[21] (B) SOUTH[22]

The causes for the high rates of unemployment, North and South, are complex and only imperfectly understood. For example, Honohan's simple model (see above) asserts that this is just reflecting the state of high British unemployment. Barry and Bradley (1991), advance more complex reasons for the South, asserting that the high natural population growth rate (with knock-on consequences for labour force growth), the high tax increases of the first half of the 1980s, and the generally depressed state of the post OPEC II world economy combined in roughly equal proportions to drive the Southern unemployment rate well above its historical parity with the British rate.

In summary, the deterioration of the Northern labour market from the late 1970s and throughout the 1980s was replicated in the South, where the overshooting of employment creation after the fiscal expansions of the late 1970s merely delayed the inevitable retribution. In both regions a serious problem of structural or long-term unemployment emerged. Economic studies in the South indicate that unemployment rose initially as a result of world recession, higher taxes and population growth pressure. Sociological studies show that a key characteristic of long-term unemployment is low skill levels, and that working class marginalization arises from the rapid and uneven nature of class transformation in Ireland and changing patterns of emigration (Breen et al. 1990).

These Southern factors clearly operated in the North as well, but were overlaid by 'community' and 'location' issues whose interpretation has been an area of great controversy in Northern socio-economic research (McGarry and O'Leary 1995). The fact that a Catholic male is still almost two and a half times more likely to be unemployed in the North than his non-Catholic counterpart may have come about for a variety of reasons in addition to claims of past or present discrimination, but certainly should direct attention to a serious Northern problem of complex origins that has been at the heart of the troubles.

3.4 PAYING THE BILLS: PUBLIC EXPENDITURE, TAXATION AND DEFICITS

The events leading up to Stormont being prorogued in 1972 may not appear to have been driven by economics, but had, in fact, many of their deeper roots in disparities of inter-community development, both real and imagined. The partial exclusion of the Catholic community from the North's governance had serious consequences for economic policy-making. In particular, most of the pre-1969 economic growth had been concentrated east of the Bann, since a passive industrial policy led naturally to firms seeking to benefit from the agglomeration economies of the greater Belfast area.[23] Even within Belfast, segmented labour markets reinforced divisions between the two main communities.

Just as the almost contemporary entry of the South into the EEC in 1973 brought in its train a wide-ranging reform and liberalization of many aspects of Southern life, so too did the imposition of direct rule facilitate labour market reforms and a greatly increased level of public expenditure aimed at raising the North to British standards of social services. However, given the previous low state of economic development in the North relative to Britain, parity of treatment, combined with the expansion of security-related expenditures, created a massive dependence on financial transfers from Britain.

After the introduction of direct rule in 1972, any attempt to maintain even an approximate link between tax revenues and public expenditures in the North was broken and public spending since then has been related to need, defined by British standards, with no local revenue raising constraint. If a regional balanced budget had continued to be required, as it was to some extent during previous decades, Canning, Moore and Rhodes (1987), suggest that some 50,000 less public sector jobs would have been sustainable, with less induced market sector employment as a consequence.

There is no disputing that the Northern economy is now a financial burden on the British Government and the region has lost its previous self-sustaining capacity.[24] The industrial sector of the North, the main source of wealth creation, has stagnated (as shown above) and the public sector is now financed through large-scale subsidies from London.[25] Estimates of this burden vary, and one set of figures for the current public deficit and the overall public sector borrowing requirement is shown in Figure 3.12(A) (with the South for comparison in Figure 3.12(B)).[26]

What these estimates show is that had the North been forced to rely on its own tax receipts, generated from its own economic activity, assuming the level of activity and all other factors remained unchanged, the result would have been a series of unsustainably large current deficits and public borrowing requirements. Had the North been an autonomous economic entity and had all other factors remained unchanged, it would have been forced into a most severe adjustment as a result of these deficits. In fact, the situation would have been worse, since the actual year-on-year regional public sector deficits do not contain any element of interest charge, as they would if they had been financed by regional-based borrowing. In reality, the position of the North within the wider UK entity and the policies pursued by British Governments, with their major redistribution dimension, meant that the North did not have to face these consequences of the hypothetical situation just considered.

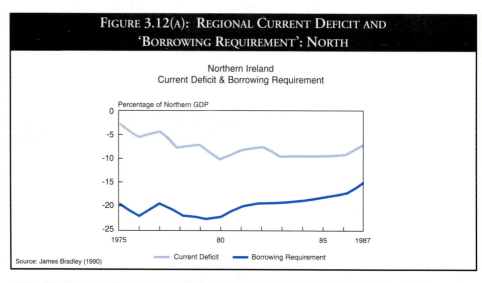

FIGURE 3.12(A): REGIONAL CURRENT DEFICIT AND 'BORROWING REQUIREMENT': NORTH

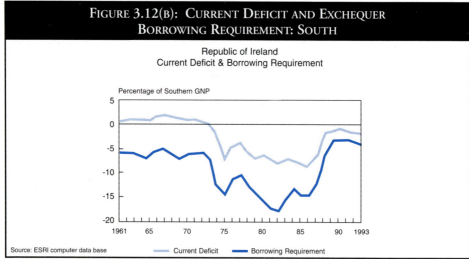

FIGURE 3.12(B): CURRENT DEFICIT AND EXCHEQUER BORROWING REQUIREMENT: SOUTH

Whereas the link between tax revenue and public expenditure in the North, considered as a separate region, has been broken, policy-makers and tax payers in the South enjoy no such luxury. For as long as British tax payers accept the current system of financing the Northern deficit, the deficit is only a residual item of limited economic consequence (McGregor et al. 1995). Furthermore, the greater than average public expenditure allocation to the North, which together with the relatively smaller Northern tax base has given rise to the need for a large subvention, could be justified on the basis of the disproportionately adverse combination of political, economic and social circumstances prevailing in the North (McNally 1995).

On the other hand, deficit-financing in the South represents a very real constraint on public policy initiatives. Prior to 1980, public expenditure in the South grew rapidly, driven mainly by an increase in public sector employment. The ratio of public to private sector employment however has been consistently lower than in the North (see Figure 3.7 above). Even as Southern tax rates were raised, the PSBR moved deeper into deficit and reached almost 16 per cent of GNP in 1981. As a consequence, the debt/GNP ratio rose and an increasing portion of this national debt was denominated in foreign currencies. This meant that interest payments on much of the debt became a direct outflow from the Southern economy and the devaluations of the Irish pound within the EMS during the first half of the 1980s further increased the debt burden.

During the early 1980s direct and indirect tax rates were raised sharply and capital expenditure curtailed, and these measures began to stabilize the national debt. However, by 1986 the Southern debt/GNP ratio rose to about 130 per cent of GNP. A further sharp adjustment was inevitable at this stage since the South had run right up against the budget constraint that the North has not yet had to face. The Southern fiscal adjustment, when it came after 1987, was extraordinarily and unexpectedly severe. Public expenditure fell, even measured in nominal terms, between 1987 and 1988. A combination of buoyant world demand, falling interest rates, and a devaluation of the Irish pound (£IR) against sterling within the EMS, boosted Southern growth and enabled the debt/GNP ratio to be cut significantly. More recently, the disciplines of the EMS (particularly prior to the broadening of the currency bands in August, 1993) and the explicit commitments in the Maastricht treaty now constrain the Southern Government from moving away, even temporarily, from fiscal rectitude.

Surprisingly, far from depressing Southern GNP, as might have been predicted by Keynesian analysis, the economy (and private consumption and investment in particular) grew very strongly in the years after the 1987 adjustment. The attention of international researchers was drawn to this apparently strange phenomenon. Giavazzi and Pagano (1991) claimed that there was actually causation underlying this correlation and argued that the South's experience during the years 1987-90 was a case of 'expansionary fiscal contraction'.[27] However, this view is controversial.[28]

Analysis of the Southern experience of fiscal restructuring should prompt reflection on the effects of a possible curtailment of the Northern subvention and how the contractionary economic effects might be offset by expansionary effects on the expectations of the private sector and by strong growth in the economies of the trading partners of the North (especially Britain and Germany).

These issues have been examined by McGregor et al. (1995), who found that there were interesting and disturbing differences between the Southern response to restructuring and possible Northern responses, based on a Scottish economic model. In the absence of a buoyant British economy, McGregor et al. found that it is very difficult for a British region to remove a regional public sector deficit. They point out, however, that the continuation of finance to fund the deficit is, of course, a purely British policy concern, not subject to the international pressures that would influence the case of similar deficits in the South (of Ireland). Table 3.1 summarizes these points.

To summarize, the Northern public sector deficit, as manifested in the need for ever larger subventions, served to sustain a high level of public and private consumption, public investment and imports. A corollary was the emergence of a chronic trade deficit, now believed to amount to between 20 and 25 per cent of regional GDP. Ironically, the South currently enjoys a trade surplus with the North of some £400 million, even though it runs a trade deficit with the whole of the UK. This is a case of beneficial spill-over from the Northern subvention. The South had embarked on a similar expansion of public expenditure in the late 1970s and early 1980s, but without the benefit of free external finance. The subsequent economic costs of restructuring were massive, but were eased in the latter part of the 1980s by a boom in the world economy.

Given the massive injection provided by the British subvention, the financing of the regional public deficit was not a problem for the North. However, the existence of the deficit (and its associated trade deficit: see below) may also be linked to an underlying problem with regional competitiveness, associated with such factors as

---

TABLE 3.1: FISCAL CUTBACKS: REGIONS AND NATIONS

National economies must pay particular attention to the sustainability of their fiscal policies. For example, the Maastricht conditions for participation in EMU place limits both on the size of a nation's public sector borrowing requirement (3 per cent of GDP) and the size of the maximum debt to GDP ratio (60 per cent)

Over the long term, in small open economies the public deficit and the deficit on the current account of the balance of payments are unavoidably interlinked. Big public deficits cause big balance of trade and of payments deficits, as in the South during the late 1970s and the first half of the 1980s.

Regions of nations are different. Those who take the expenditure and tax decisions which result in regional deficits also take the decision (at least implicitly) to finance them: sustainability in a regional context is simply about the political will of the national government to maintain transfers from the rest of the national government to the deficit region.

The national government's willingness to finance a deficit region depends on non-economic factors (such as a desire for national cohesion), but is influenced by economic factors such as 'the importance of being unimportant' (e.g., the North is small relative to Britain), and 'the importance of being unnoticed' (e.g., the Northern subvention can be clearly identified because of the manner in which the region relates to the national authority; Scottish or Welsh deficits are more difficult to measure).

---

the sectoral coverage of Northern manufacturing, the continued concentration on the British market, and close links between British and Northern wages and costs. The fact that the South emerged from a similar case of twin deficits during the 1980s may hold interesting lessons for future Northern transformation.

3.5 REGIONAL EXPENDITURE, COMPETITIVENESS AND THE TRADE BALANCE

In large relatively closed economies the expenditure breakdown of GNP into its separate components is of central concern. For example, in the British economy the role played by private consumption and private house purchase in overheating the economy in the late 1980s is being followed by a preoccupation with a consumer-led recovery in the 1990s. Indeed, there has been a tendency to interpret the Northern Ireland experience during the recent UK recession as a milder version of essentially the same type of wider national recession (Gudgin and O'Shea 1992).

In their analysis of the Northern experience of recession, Gudgin and O'Shea (1993) place great emphasis on consumer spending, in particular the influence of house prices and access to consumer credit on household behaviour. Three factors are advanced to account for the lower amplitude of cyclical fluctuations in Northern Ireland and the consequential mildness of the recent Northern recession:

- The absence of a speculative property boom equivalent to that of Britain between 1986 and 1989;

- The relatively larger Northern public sector, although this is largely discounted as an explanation by Gudgin and O'Shea;

- The lower exposure of Northern manufacturing to the depressed British markets and a wage-cost competitive advantage.

However, the Northern Ireland Economic Council (NIEC) has interpreted the latter two of these factors as representing an underlying structural weakness which may be further exacerbated when the British economy moves into its recovery cycle (NIEC 1993). Furthermore, an excessively strong focus on the behaviour of internal regional consumer demand is not appropriate to the economic circumstances of a regional economy that is as open as the North.[29] Southern analysts, in their efforts to isolate the primary medium-term driving forces of the South's economy, place much more emphasis on the primary role of external forces and the performance of the supply side of the exposed trading sector (with the downstream secondary consequences, of course, for domestic demand) than on the behaviour of private consumption and private housing investment. Domestic demand factors are important, but their significance in the medium to long term is more as 'effects' rather than 'causes' in the economies of the North and South (see Bradley, FitzGerald and McCoy 1991).

Until the mid-1970s the UK Regional Accounts contained data on imports into and exports from the North. Although no official trade data are available after 1974 — a disappointing situation, given the previous record of regional data collection — unofficial estimates can be made. For example, Rowthorn, 1987 provides output-expenditure estimates for selected years in the period 1970-84 from which it is possible to calculate a residual net trade balance. Using available time series data, we have also made such estimates, and the resulting net trade balance is shown in Figure 3.13 as a percentage of Northern GDP.[30] It is seen that the Northern trade balance was almost in equilibrium in the early 1970s, just prior to the OPEC I recession and before the civil unrest became serious. Subsequently there was a sharp deterioration that has persisted to the present day.

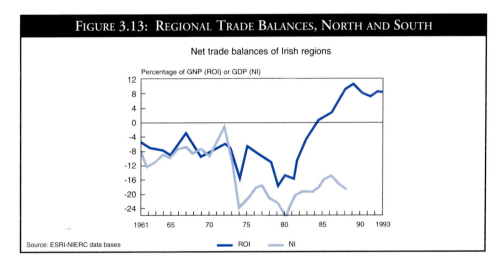

FIGURE 3.13: REGIONAL TRADE BALANCES, NORTH AND SOUTH

Net trade balances of Irish regions

Source: ESRI-NIERC data bases

ROI   NI

The situation in a small open regional economy is very different from the large economy case. Such a region is so dependent on its export markets that the operation of the supply-side of the economy is of primary concern, rather than the demand side. Here the difference between the North, as a region of the UK, and the South, as a sovereign State, becomes crucial. It is obvious that the Southern balance of trade and the current and capital accounts of the balance of payments place constraints on private sector behaviour and the operation of public policy. So, for example, when the excessively high public expenditure of the late 1970s and early 1980s led to deterioration of both the public sector borrowing requirement (with a consequential rapid accumulation of public debt) and of the current account of the balance of payments, severe constraints were placed on public policy (Figure 3.14).

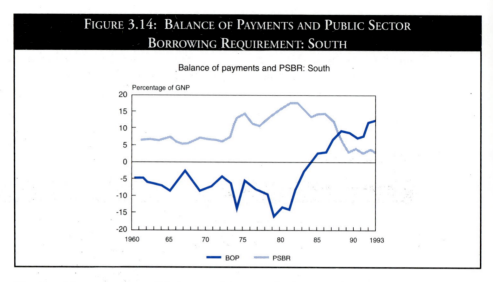

FIGURE 3.14: BALANCE OF PAYMENTS AND PUBLIC SECTOR BORROWING REQUIREMENT: SOUTH

The South's macro-disequilibrium problems took almost a decade to bring under control and continue to constrain the role of public policy during the 1990s. This story is well known and need not be laboured (Bradley et al. 1985; FitzGerald 1986). Conversely, the South's trade surplus that emerged in the late 1980s and endures to the present, is distorted by transfer pricing, i.e., the behaviour of foreign multinationals who mark up the input costs of their Irish branches to increase the fraction of their global output that is subject to the low Irish tax regime rather than the higher regime of the parent country (mainly the US).

The parallel problems of the implications of the Northern trade deficits are quite different from the South. On the one hand, the problems are less serious for the Northern economy simply because responsibility for any notional Northern element of a UK balance of payments deficit rests with the British Government and not with the Northern Ireland authorities. However, the feedback from an adverse regional balance of trade is likely to be bound up in the way in which a sovereign nation like the UK handles regional policy and inter-regional transfers. In the case of the North, there are interesting parallels with the Mezzogiorno region of Italy, where fiscal integration and large-scale public transfers have led to the decline of the traded sector and to a state of semi-permanent dependency and underdevelopment (CEC 1993). We return to this issue later.

Northern exposure to Britain as a destination for its external sales of manufactured goods (34 per cent) is about twice as high as Southern export exposure to Britain

(15 per cent), where both are measured in terms of the fraction of their regional output sold in Britain.[31] Based on the survey data of Scott and O'Reilly (1992), Figure 3.15(A) shows the destination of all sales of Northern manufactured goods in the year 1990, and 3.15(B) shows the equivalent data for the South, based on the 1990 Census of Industrial Production. It is seen that the North has an exposure amounting to 72 per cent of sales of manufactured goods within the economy of these two islands, while the corresponding figure for the South is at the lower level of 55 per cent.[32]

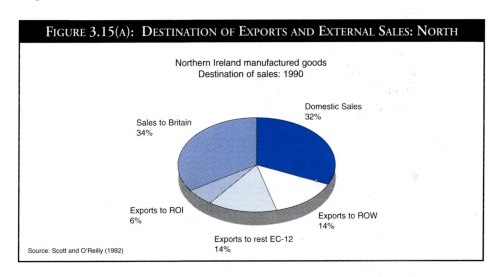

FIGURE 3.15(A): DESTINATION OF EXPORTS AND EXTERNAL SALES: NORTH

Northern Ireland manufactured goods
Destination of sales: 1990

Domestic Sales
32%

Sales to Britain
34%

Exports to ROI
6%

Exports to rest EC-12
14%

Exports to ROW
14%

Source: Scott and O'Reilly (1992)

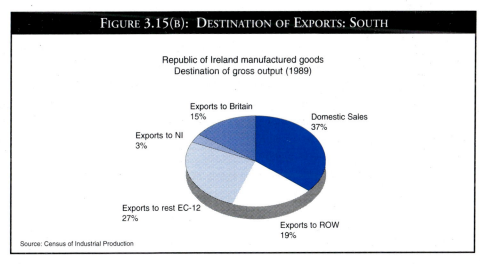

FIGURE 3.15(B): DESTINATION OF EXPORTS: SOUTH

Republic of Ireland manufactured goods
Destination of gross output (1989)

Exports to Britain
15%

Exports to NI
3%

Domestic Sales
37%

Exports to rest EC-12
27%

Exports to ROW
19%

Source: Census of Industrial Production

The emergence of such a large and persistent balance of trade deficit in the South would be symptomatic of a deeply uncompetitive regional economy. However, the position in the North is rather different. Although there has been considerable evidence of an underlying problem with cost competitiveness in the North (Borooah and Lee 1991), the trade deficit is also a direct consequence of the massive external financing of the Northern public sector deficit by means of the annual subvention from Britain. Indeed, the two explanatory factors — poor cost competitiveness and the need for external subvention financing — are intimately linked.

The South's data for North-South trade illustrates the emergence of the large trade deficit run by the North with the South, as shown in Figure 3.16. Prior to the 1960s, the balance had been in favour of the North, but a modest deficit emerged during the 1960s and 1970s, a time when the South itself moved towards a serious balance of trade deficit with the rest of the world. However, a significant trade deficit in favour of the South emerged in the early 1980s, and has persisted to the present. It now amounts to between £IR 300 and £IR 400 million, i.e., between 1 and 2 per cent of Southern GNP.[33]

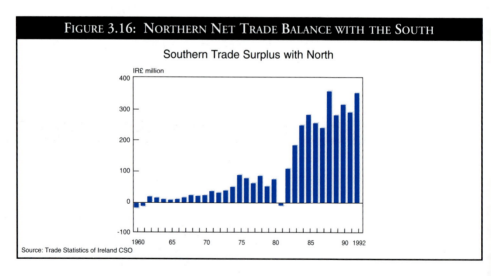

FIGURE 3.16: NORTHERN NET TRADE BALANCE WITH THE SOUTH

Southern Trade Surplus with North

IR£ million

Source: Trade Statistics of Ireland CSO

Based on these data, Scott and O'Reilly (1992) draw some interesting, if pessimistic, conclusions on the prospects for faster Northern and Southern growth based on greater trade penetration, as stated in the May 1990 CII newsletter. They point out that the existing level of sales between the two regions of Ireland appears to be largely in line with the level of sales between other small European countries and their nearest neighbours. While they do not rule out all benefits of greater North-South trade penetration, their estimate of the likely job gains, at 7,500, is only one tenth of the CII estimate of 75,000.[34]

3.6 COSTING THE TROUBLES

If a firm or an entire economy undergoes an unexpected serious decline, and if the causes of that decline can be clearly identified to the satisfaction of everybody, then the task of policy-makers in the private and public sectors becomes much easier, should they wish to design and implement policies to reverse the decline.

What were the reasons for the reversal of growth and sharp decline in Northern manufacturing performance in the 1970s, a performance that is in stark contrast to the relative success of the South? Three potential causes can be suggested immediately:

1. The troubles, which became serious at just the time the decline in manufacturing employment started to get serious;

2. The weakening of regional and industrial policy in the UK, particularly after the election of a Conservative Government in 1979;

3. The slower growth in the world economy that followed the OPEC I and OPEC II world recessions.

In order to examine these hypotheses one tries to conceptualize a situation where some or all of the potential factors causing the economic decline take different paths from those of the historical record. Thus, for example, one might try to imagine a world where there had been no OPEC oil crises, or one where the troubles had never broken out in the North. Comparing the historical economic out-turn (i.e., with the troubles and the OPEC recessions factored in) to the hypothetical or counter factual case (i.e., without the troubles or the OPEC recessions) should permit the impact of the troubles and the OPEC recessions to be identified.[35]

Analysis based on a simple counter factual technique was used by Moore and Rhodes (1973), to evaluate the impact of regional industrial development assistance policies on the North over the 1960s and the 1970s. The approach has three stages:

1. Assume each Northern industry grows at the aggregate UK industry rate, and define this as causing an expected level of employment (E) as distinct from the actual level (A).

2. Divide the period into a (prior) 'policy off' period and an active 'policy on' period. Extrapolate the 'policy off' evolution of the difference between E and A above into the 'policy on' period.

3. The effect of the operation of regional policies during the 'policy on' period is derived by comparing the actual Northern-UK difference (from 1 above) and the hypothetical extrapolated Northern-UK difference (from 2 above).

Using this approach, Harris (1991, 70-73) suggested that between 1960 and 1971 an extra 33,000 jobs were created in the North through the operation of regional industrial policies, but by 1983 the net increase had fallen to zero. However, Harris is critical of this approach for two reasons:

- The methodology assumes a zero-sum game, where extra jobs in the North are at the expense of jobs elsewhere in the UK.

- The methodology produces a catch-all, and is unable to distinguish component policy effects or other non-policy influences, such as the three listed above.

The approach was modified by Harris to take account of the troubles in the North as follows. For the period prior to the troubles (1961-69), the difference between actual and expected performance for Northern Ireland (from 1 above) is compared with the differences for the other development assistance areas of Britain, and a formal statistical relationship is derived. This relationship is then used to predict a hypothetical 'no troubles' scenario for the subsequent period 1970-83 for Northern Ireland on the assumption that changes in the relative effectiveness of policy in the North and in the other British Development Areas would have been exactly the same in the 1970s in the absence of the civil unrest. Hence, *all* Northern underperformance in manufacturing employment is attributed to the civil unrest.

The results of this analysis suggest that NI regional policy created some 22,000 net new jobs between 1960 and 1983, and that the civil unrest was responsible for the loss of about the same number of jobs (Harris 1991, 164-165). Similar estimates have been derived using this methodology by the Northern Ireland Economic Research Centre (NIERC 1990) and Rowthorn (1987). However, Harris points out the dangers of attributing all of the post-1969 difference between developments in British assisted areas and Northern Ireland to the troubles. Other factors could have been at work, such as lower Northern efficiency and cost competitiveness, and the effects of the troubles may have been minimal (Harris 1991, 165).

A second much simpler approach narrows the focus to the public expenditure aspects that are most directly related to the troubles, such as policing, military, prisons, etc. (Tomlinson 1994; DKM 1994). So, for example, a counter factual assumption is made that in the absence of the troubles the level of security expenditure in the North would have been similar, on a per capita basis, say to that in the rest of Britain. The difference between the (low) counter factual security and the (high) actual expenditure is assigned to be the 'cost' of the troubles for this particular element of public expenditure.

Both approaches have serious problems. The first (economy wide) approach tends to explain every difference between the counter factual and the actual as being troubles-related, even when there may have been other important factors at work that were quite unrelated to the troubles. The second (narrow public finance) approach may simply miss wider economic disruptions that could have caused more damage than the higher level of troubles-related public expenditure. Applications of the second approach have also been used to identify the public expenditure peace dividend, basically by using the no troubles counter factual to estimate public expenditure savings for the future, rather than public expenditure costs for the past (NIEC, 1995). Obviously all such peace dividend estimates suffer from the same problems as the troubles estimates.

In spite of all the research that has been carried out on the Northern economy before and during the troubles, our review of the literature on 'costing' the troubles leads us to the conclusion that no firm answers can be given to questions concerning the relative contributions of the three causes of slower Northern growth and poorer performance that we listed at the start of this section. The published direct analysis of the impact of the troubles on the whole economy, on sectors or on the public finances in isolation, is seriously flawed and cannot be reliably used to isolate the troubles from wider factors. The same applies to attempts to analyse the contribution of changes in UK regional policy regimes that came about in the late 1970s and during the 1980s. Finally, the absence of widely accepted and reliable economic models of the Northern economy have made it difficult to study the impact on the North of economic developments in the rest of the world.

PART II
POLICY STRUCTURES AND THE SOCIO-ECONOMIC CONTEXT

4 ECONOMIC POLICY STRUCTURES ON THE ISLAND

4.1 ECONOMICS AND POLITICS

Although the North enjoyed some policy autonomy in fiscal and public expenditure areas prior to 1972 under the Stormont parliament, today the Northern authorities have only limited discretion on regional economic policy. Monetary policy in the North, and almost all elements of taxation and public expenditure policy, are set by UK norms, although there remains some discretion in the area of regional industrial policy.

The South, on the other hand, always had the potential for extensive freedom for independent policy actions, although we have noted in chapter 2 that this was not regularly exercized in practice. For example, the South maintained a fixed link with sterling for almost six decades after independence, only breaking this link after EMS entry in 1979.[1] However, in the area of industrial policy, with an emphasis on attracting foreign direct investment (FDI), the South deviated considerably from UK corporate tax norms from the mid 1950s onwards. Nevertheless, EU membership, the imperatives of tax harmonization within Europe, and the Maastricht guidelines, now place tight constraints on present and future Southern domestic fiscal and monetary policy. The more recent broadening of the EMS currency bands has freed these constraints only to a limited degree and present Southern policy is predicated on joining the core EMU countries at the first feasible opportunity.

The task of exploring future Irish economic policy perspectives in the context of a peaceful Northern Ireland is fraught with practical and conceptual difficulties. For

economy would be unable to support the present level of subvention, making political reunification a decidedly unattractive economic proposition to nationalists, even if it were feasible.[4] Even if a form of Northern independence were acceptable to nationalists, it would have to be ruled out for the foreseeable future on economic grounds. It is simply inconceivable that the necessary funding for the subvention, required to maintain standards of living at or near the levels to which people have become accustomed and will wish to retain, could be obtained from other sources, either in the form of transfers or sovereign borrowing by the North.

If hypothetically, however, the North were required by the British Government to function within a much smaller subvention (say 2 to 3 per cent of regional GDP, the present range of the South's public sector borrowing requirement), and were required to adjust to that lower level fairly quickly, then there would have to be a drastic deflation, involving sizeable cuts in the level and quality of all Northern public services. In such rather improbable circumstances, nationalist attitudes to greater North-South linkages might be very different.

Unionist attitudes to Northern economic dependence are much more straightforward, but not without problems. For unionists the North is now, and must always remain, within the UK. For them, being a region of the UK carries with it an automatic guarantee of parity in the quality of public services. Having started from a lower base, and having experienced exceptional economic difficulties during the troubles, the unionists feel it quite natural that the North requires a period of 'catch-up', during which it will be entitled to attract a greater per capita subvention than other more prosperous UK regions. Furthermore, this dependence on transfers from Britain acts as a bulwark against any possibility of a united Ireland, given the inability and/or unwillingness of the Southern tax payer to take over the present subvention, and thus sustain the higher Northern standard of living. The ultimate expression of this point of view is one of surprise that the South ever felt the need to leave the Union and divorce itself from these economic benefits (Cadogan Group 1993; Roche and Birnie 1995).

Thus, from a strictly economic point of view there appear to be only limited differences in attitudes between unionists and nationalists towards continuation of the British-financed subvention. However, the political implications for each group are very different. For unionists, acceptance of the subvention is an economic expression of a desire for continued incorporation of the North within the UK. However, for nationalists a willingness to enjoy the fruits of a higher standard of living permitted by the British-financed subvention clearly creates dissonance with a desire for a greater Irish dimension to Northern governance. In a hypothetical situation where the subvention finance from Britain were to be drastically cut, unionist attitudes to closer formal policy relationships with the South would be unlikely to change. However, there would probably be a much greater willingness on the part of nationalists to turn to the South for whatever offsetting economic benefits such links might bring.[5]

Indeed, if the North had continued to function under the type of financial constraints that applied earlier under Stormont, it is quite likely that the standard of living in both regions of Ireland would have converged during the 1970s and 1980s, to a level below that of Britain and a fortiori below that of the main EU members. We can only guess at the nature of the pressures that might have emerged in the North, either for greater policy independence along Southern lines, or for a negotiated form of full integration into the UK that may have differed from imposed direct rule.

4.2 THE NATURE OF ECONOMIC GOVERNANCE

Every way one turns in the North, politics and economics are intertwined. Thus, in order to explore the full range of possible economic implications of a permanent peace, it is necessary to examine a variety of North-South economic policy configurations. Such configurations carry with them profound political implications, the treatment of which goes far beyond this study.[6] Ideally, the examination of economic policy aspects should be carried out in tandem with the political and institutional consultative process and not, as here, separate from that process and in the absence of even the start of formal all-party talks on the future of the North. Nevertheless, it may be helpful to explore economic policy principles and key strategies that should inform responses to the peace process by carrying out a range of ex ante thought experiments, however provocative they may appear to some of the participants in that process.

By the term economic governance we mean the manner in which the full range of economic policies is implemented in a State or arranged between States. The distinction between political and economic governance arises quite naturally within the European Union, where many treaties deal mainly with economic policy. Similarly, Southern relations with the UK have sometimes concerned economic governance, the Anglo-Irish Free Trade Agreement of 1965 being a case in point. However, it is not such a familiar notion in North-South relations.

In identifying different options for economic governance we focus mainly on one aspect of the problem: namely, the nature of North-South relationships. In adopting such a focus, we assert that the North-South axis is as important as another obvious alternative, namely the East-West axis. In this terminology we use East-West to encompass the relationship of both Irish regions with the EU, with Britain and with the rest of the world. The North-South axis encompasses the relationships of the two regional economies on this island with each other. On the face of it, this may appear to be an unrealistic, if not downright foolish, claim. In the following material and chapters we hope to justify it.

Our concentration on a North-South focus is perfectly consistent with the fact that the major external markets and sources of inward investment for both regions presently lie, and will continue to lie, outside this island. It is also consistent with the fact that even in the case of a 'single island economy', Ireland would still have one of the most open economies in the world. But openness in terms of trade, in a situation where island production is dominated by foreign multinational branch plants, is not a position of strength. Resolution of economic problems on the North-South axis could be considered to be a necessary condition for encouraging growth of strong indigenous firms, including Irish multinationals. But unless islandwide commercial opportunities are embraced with enthusiasm, and the full potential of the island within the dynamic EU and world economies is exploited to the full, resolution of problems on the North-South axis will hardly be a *sufficient* precondition for a strong island economy.

We identify three broad alternatives for the future evolution of economic policy for the two regions of Ireland in a period of permanent peace: separate development; coordinated development; and a single island economy. Since we are concerned mainly with the North-South policy axis, these three stylized options are conceptualized to differ mainly in the nature and strength of North-South policy interaction.

Our category of *separate development* is intended to explore a situation where there is very limited or no formal policy coordination between the two regions of the island. Thus, it is consistent with a continuation of the status quo (i.e., direct rule), full integration of the North into the UK, or with a fully independent North.

The *single island economy* option is at the other extreme, with a comprehensive policy harmonization of a type that would only be conceivable in a confederal, federal or united Ireland or possibly within a federal post-EMU European Union. The intermediate case, *coordinated development*, allows for a hybrid outcome of partial policy coordination, that would be consistent with the North remaining within the UK, but with devolved power over a wide range of policy instruments that was operated in cooperation with the South and with the consent of the British Government.

Most previous studies of possible future Northern constitutional arrangements have tended to focus mainly on political/institutional issues rather than on economic policy matters. For example, O'Leary, Lyne, Marshall and Rowthorn (1993) examine five such options: full integration into the UK; unification within the Republic of Ireland; Northern independence; re-partition; and shared authority (the preferred option of the authors). Only in cases two and three (unification and independence) are economic factors the main negative element in rejecting the option.[7] The New Ireland Forum study of macroeconomic consequences of integrated economic policy in Ireland, carried out by the consultants DKM, basically costed the public finance implications of three main political options: a unitary State; a federal/confederal State; and joint authority. Relatively little consideration was given to the wider economic policy potentials of the different political options.[8]

4.3 ALTERNATIVE FORMS OF ECONOMIC GOVERNANCE

Economic governance concerns the manner in which the full range of economic policies is implemented in a State or between States. These include fiscal policy (public expenditure and taxation), monetary policy (interest rates and exchange rates), labour market policy (wage setting arrangements, education and training, etc.), regional policy (infrastructure and physical planning), and a wide variety of sectoral policies in areas such as agriculture (controlled to a large extent by the CAP) and industry (grants, incentives, promotion of inward investment).

These policies can seldom be operated in isolation from each other, but are closely interrelated through the operation of the public sector budget constraint. Thus, for example, the operation of an industrial incentive scheme based on low corporate tax rates might require offsetting high rates of personal income tax; adherence to the narrow band of the EMS would require accomodating tight wage policies to preserve cost competitiveness; improvement in regional infrastructure might require less public expenditure in social areas.

Furthermore, all policies operate under constraints. Membership of the EU requires forgoing tariffs on trade, restrictions on how indirect taxes such as VAT are set, and controls on other policies that are deemed to interfere with fair competition (e.g., the requirement to abolish the zero tax rate on manufactured exports in the South and replace it by a flat 10 per cent corporation tax rate on profits in manufacturing). Domestic political considerations also place constraints on policy, e.g. on the level of taxes, as in the tax revolts in the South in the early 1980s. Finally, constraints arise from the structure of the economy and its relationship with other economies. For example, the high rates of excise duty in the South during the 1980s induced such a high level of cross-border shopping/smuggling as to place an effective cap on the level of such taxes. High rates of personal income tax in the South also tend to be associated with outward migration flows of skilled labour.

At a superficial level, the South has considerably more policy autonomy than the North. However, at a more fundamental level, any such autonomy is highly constrained. Thus, the public expenditure increases of the late 1970s and early 1980s produced short-run gains in growth and employment but were choked off and reversed in the longer run due to the resulting large public sector borrowing requirements and the accompanying balance of payments deficits. Attempts to generate increased tax revenue by raising tax rates, and thus control the escalating public sector debt, further exacerbated the resulting recession.[9]

In the North policies are set mainly according to UK norms. Thus, while tax rates in the North are identical to the UK level, rates of expenditure can be set with some limited discretion within a block grant to the Northern Ireland Office. Examples where this discretion is used include industrial incentives and education expenditure. Nevertheless, the fact remains that policy norms in the North are those designed with the wider UK in mind, and can be unsuitable for a peripheral region.[10] While the subvention assistance can be used to operate beneficial policies to address the North's structural problems, some of these problems may originate in the application of UK-wide policies to the North.

The dilemma of regions of sovereign States as they participate in the global economy has been the subject of reflections by Ohmae (1994), who holds that the nation State has become an unnatural, sometimes dysfunctional, unit for organizing human activity and managing economic endeavour in a borderless world. He contends that it sometimes represents no genuine, shared community of economic interests; it defines no meaningful flows of economic activity. In fact, it overlooks the true linkages and synergies that exist among often disparate populations by combining important measures of human activity at the wrong level of analysis. Within the UK, both Northern Ireland and Scotland have displayed the tensions that Ohmae generalizes. Within these islands, Britain and the South (of Ireland) display the opposite problem: a reluctance based on their past history to engage deeply in the type of close inter-country political-economic cooperation that characterizes, for example, the EU in general and the Benelux region in particular.[11] Although the legacy of the pre-1920 Union endures in many areas of Southern Irish life, the dynamic of future political-economic integration seems to lie more with the EU than between these two neigbouring islands, in a context where the present British reluctance to engage positively in the European debate is well known.[12]

4.3.1 SEPARATE DEVELOPMENT

Separate development is essentially the institutional situation which prevailed before the ceasefires, with only modest North-South economic interaction and limited formal policy coordination. It is the conceptual background to economic forecasts prepared before the ceasefires (Cantillon, Curtis and FitzGerald 1994; Gudgin and O'Shea 1993), for many studies of the costs of the troubles to the two Irish regions and to Britain (DKM 1994), and to much of the analysis of the economic potential that peace might bring (NIEC 1995; KPMG 1995). Being the most familiar North-South policy stance, this option forms a type of benchmark, against which any policy evolution must be judged.

Until quite recently economic forecasts were prepared, North and South, with literally no reference to the other region. This was due in part to the relative insignificance of North-South interactions when compared with, say, the relationship of both regions with Britain and with the rest of the European Union. However, it was also conditioned by a lack of formal economic and market research on the modest, but none the less important, ways in which both regions have interacted in the past. Worse, it may have been conditioned by simple ignorance of potentials for greater interaction that have been fuelled by gross misconceptions about the past and recent history of both regions.[13]

Two different costs associated with violence have been considered under the heading of separate development, with their mirror images of potential benefits of peace as these costs are reduced or vanish altogether. First, there are the obvious costs, in terms of deaths, human injury, material damage, extra security expenditure, disruption of normal business life, and the like. Economists and actuaries are obliged to put monetary values on deaths and injuries, but such costings are a grossly inadequate proxy for the unacceptable human misery caused by twenty five years of paramilitary violence (Stationery Office 1983b; DKM 1994). Second, there are the hidden costs, such as previous growth potential not realized, failure to attract foreign direct investment, stunted tourism growth, and so on. The former costs are not negligible, and were estimated by DKM (in 1989 prices) at about £365 per capita annually in the North and £225 per capita in the South. However, they are probably overshadowed by the second type of costs, which represent a more direct loss to the island, rather than a diversion of public expenditure away from productive activities.

Under the separate development alternative, it is important to correct some misunderstandings about the costs of violence, and the consequential benefits of peace. We showed in chapter 3 that not all of the accelerated decline of Northern manufacturing during the 1970s was caused by violence, since the composition of Northern manufacturing was such that a serious shake-out was inevitable in any event. However, the inability of the North to substitute 'sunrise' for 'sunset' industries is probably largely attributable to the violence, as comparison with Scotland and the Republic shows (NIEC 1992; Hamilton 1995).

Nor can the rise in the Northern subvention be regarded as a 'cost' of violence, in this case one to be borne by the British tax payer. Even if Stormont had survived to the present day, it is difficult to see how a massive rise in net transfers from the other British regions to the North could have been avoided. An important aspect of future UK Government policy towards the North must be to send clear signals about the future of the subvention. For example, in his speech to the Institute of Directors in Belfast on 21 October 1994, the Prime Minister John Major gave an assurance that: '... the Government will take full account of Northern Ireland's special needs in setting future levels of public expenditure for the province.' This may mean that any savings in expenditure on security are likely to be recycled to other areas, designed to boost activity in the private sector in addition to augmenting deserving areas of the already large public sector. Nevertheless, it may eventually appear desirable to reduce the role played by the subvention and encourage growth of private sector activity. If not, there is a risk that the North will be locked into a semi-permanent dependency that, however comfortable in the short term, can hardly be economically healthy or wise in the long term.

Any restructuring of the subvention would also be of considerable interest and concern to the South. At present the Northern economy is dominated by its trade, investment and other links with Britain. The Southern economy, on the other hand, has diversified away from a similar dominance during the last three decades and is now more internationally oriented. However, we saw in chapter 3 that the Southern trade surplus with the North, at about £400 million, is an important by-product of the subvention that sustains Southern jobs.

A crucial issue for the future is whether the previous pattern of separate economic development will continue to be thought to be the best choice for the future, or whether these weak links can be developed to become an additional force for mutually reinforcing growth in the island economy. Nevertheless, most recent studies of the future of the island have tended either to be silent on the exact scope for beneficial North-South policy interaction (NIGC 1995), or are actively hostile to the development of any such policy interaction (Cadogan Group 1995; Roche and Birnie 1995). We return to the substantive issues raised in these reports later in chapter 6.

It must be stressed that a situation of separate policy development between North and South is rapidly becoming artificial and outdated. We formulated the concept in the negative way we did simply to emphasize the historically inherited situation rather example, one obvious possibility is that peace might simply facilitate a resumption of business as usual, where the North continues to be a region of the UK (like, say, Scotland or East Anglia), with no provision for formal North-South political or economic policy structures. At another extreme the North might eventually evolve towards forms of greater political and economic independence, acquiring considerably more regional policy autonomy than at present. If such an arrangement came to pass, an independent North might choose to exercise its autonomy by negotiating formal North-South structures of mutual benefit to both regions that might ultimately lead to a form of confederation, federation or unification. A wide range of variations lying between these polar cases would also be possible.

Although the above range of possibilities provides food for interesting economic speculation, a fundamental difficulty with any such reflections has been stated very bluntly by McGarry and O'Leary (1995):

> The Northern Ireland conflict has been waged paramilitarily and politically between two communities with different national identities, not between two aggregates of individuals mainly interested in promoting their economic wellbeing. (P. 306.)

Hence, the very limited extent to which economic policy choices can be divorced from political arrangements restricts the scope for productive speculation on the future economics of the two regions of the island, and a full separation of these two aspects of governance requires an act of faith that history tells us is probably unrealistic.[2]

To illustrate this dilemma, consider the picture of the Northern economy that emerges from chapter 3, i.e., one where the economic prosperity that the region undoubtedly enjoys (relative to the South) is presently underwritten to a large degree by the British tax payer. The size of the public sector, and the role played by transfers to persons and companies, appears to have engendered a situation of economic dependence that goes considerably further than its Southern counterpart. However, Northern attitudes to this benign form of dependence take different forms, depending on one's political and cultural affiliation.

For nationalists, one aspect of a continued economic dependence of the North on the British tax payer is that they need to work out their economic aspirations in the short to medium term within the political context of the UK.[3] The Southern than to ignore very recent developments. Whether they like it or not, Northern and Southern public policy-makers are coming under increasing pressures from the private business sectors of both regions to harmonize a range of key policies on a cross-border basis, in areas such as tourism, physical infrastructure, telecommunications, energy, etc. This brings us naturally to the notion of coordinated policy-making, to which we now turn.

4.3.2 COORDINATED DEVELOPMENT

Coordinated development assumes an increased level of cooperation in areas such as tourism, cross-border infrastructure planning, and industrial policy to attract foreign investment and encourage the growth of indigenous industry and services.[14] Hence, this process would involve the harmonization of a subset of public policies, thus needing explicit political agreement and political structures that go beyond those that have operated over the past ten years. Some such coordination could conceivably take place spontaneously through the intervention of individual private firms and business organizations. However, as we will discuss below, there are areas of policy *failure* on the island, where many of the problems are of a macroeconomic or macro-sectoral kind that the private sector is likely to be ill-equipped to deal with adequately.

Policy coordination would also need the goodwill of the Northern and Southern private sectors, as expressed through their organizations and trades unions. However, coordinated development of policy is increasingly seen by the business community, North and South, as a logical and efficient way of exploiting the strengths of the island's human and physical resources (Coopers & Lybrand/Indecon 1994). Such arrangements are also envisaged in the Framework Document, albeit somewhat tentatively and in a context where the economic logic, although given its place, is probably secondary to political considerations.

The option of coordinated development could involve many different institutional forms. For example, responsibility for coordination of North-South matters could be operated by the Governments of the South and of the UK alone; by the Government of the South and public authorities in the North, operating in conjunction with the British Government; or by the Government of the South in cooperation with autonomous authorities in the North, within terms of reference agreed between the Southern and UK Governments.

The crucial aspect of this option is a quest for the maximum amount of beneficial policy coordination consistent with the broad maintenance of the present constitutional position of the North as a region of the United Kingdom. O'Leary et al. (1993) have explored a form of shared authority that would appear to be consistent with this constitutional objective. However, under coordinated development the fiscal and monetary arrangements in the North would continue to be set within the United Kingdom, and thus the process stops short of the notion of island EMU.

Many economic reasons could be advanced to justify in principle a greater level of future North-South policy coordination. At the local level, the EU INTERREG programme recognizes the particular problems experienced by cross-border areas throughout the EU, where the natural links that emerge between regions within a sovereign State are disrupted by international land borders. The principle of subsidiarity does not appear to work well in this area of policy formation, and has been actively encouraged by formal EU programmes.

At a higher level of regional and national policy-making involving the North and South there are many issues such as policy externalities and spillovers that are not handled well under the present institutional framework. Examples include matters that intrinsically concern the island as a unit, such as tourism promotion, planning of physical infrastructure, energy and telecommunications policy, promoting mutually beneficial business linkages, etc.

For example, any marketing of the South as a tourist destination will almost certainly generate extra business for the North as well, and vice versa. Indeed, the troubles prevented an earlier joint exploitation of what is pre-eminently an integrated island tourist potential. Conversely, of course, the Northern troubles undoubtedly generated negative spill over effects for the South, as the British tourist trade to the South collapsed after 1969, and as potential tourists reacted to worldwide negative images of Northern violence and the consequent oppressive military and police presence.

Similarly, road, rail and telecommunication investment programmes become difficult to coordinate across an international border, and particularly so between North and South. The negative externalities of non-cooperative infrastructure planning in the areas of North-South road and rail links have been recently documented by Smyth

(1995, 165-185). Energy planning for a small island divided into two different political jurisdictions has made it difficult to plan electricity generating stations of a minimum efficient size.

The above examples are typical of a wide range of areas where the presence of positive and negative externalities and spill overs point strongly to the desirability of better standards of North-South policy cooperation. There appears to be no economic reason why such cooperation should not evolve over time, either bilaterally on an Anglo-Irish basis or within the context of the EU. However, it is more difficult to see such cooperation extending easily to potentially competitive areas such as the attraction of foreign industry to locate North or South, or the encouragement of harmonization in the wide range of social and educational policies on the island.

Indeed, the absence of fiscal and monetary harmonization introduces a potentially serious North-South complication, particularly if the UK deviates from evolving European consensus on economic and social harmonization. The problem here is that the North is a region of the UK, and the South is a sovereign State. Hence, the present constitutional situation means that North-South policy harmonization boils down to harmonization between the UK and the South (of Ireland). The South has participated more enthusiastically in EU policy areas than the UK, for example joining the EMS narrow band of currencies in 1978 at a time when the UK opted out. The irony is that the role of the EU has brought policy disruption rather than policy harmonization in some of the South's most important economic relationships with the UK.[15]

Just as the Single European Market and EMU contains an internal logic of further integration, so too a process of North-South coordinated development is likely to lead inexorably to suggestions for further harmonization and policy convergence. Even within the UK, strains have already emerged due to the higher level of grants offered by the North to attract foreign industry where other British firms feel threatened. The recent controversy over a Far East textiles plant is a case where the debate actually led to British textile manufacturers challenging the level of Northern aid through the European Court. Given such intra-UK disputes, it is doubtful if North-South policy coordination could succeed other than within a long-term commitment to complete harmonization of policy on the island, perhaps within the context of the EU.

The term coordinated development is intended to go much further in order to address areas of market failure such as physical infrastructure, and missing markets (such as the separate Northern and Southern product distribution systems). In addition, there are other areas of policy-making where differences between the South and the UK tend to create an uneven North-South playing field (e.g., industrial incentives such as the low Southern rate of corporation tax in manufacturing and the high rates of direct subsidies offered in Britain and in the North). However, in this case the process of islandwide coordination may involve a trade-off for both North and South, where any gains from North-South harmonization may impose costs as Northern policy deviates from Britain and/or Southern policy harmonizes with Britain.

It has been suggested that the evolution of North-South economic cooperation should be left to market forces, thus eliminating any requirement for formal inter-Governmental policy coordination bodies. This low key approach has been advocated by Roche and Birnie, (1995, 41) who assert that the Northern and Southern private sectors should be allowed decide for themselves what kind of efforts are advantageous and necessary. Of course these types of low key interactions are already in train in many areas (e.g., all-Ireland tourism promotion, joint trade missions to foreign markets, joint IBEC/CBI(NI) initiatives, etc.).

Nevertheless, the experience of the EU has been that a strong commitment by governments is needed to harmonize policy, remove non-tariff barriers to trade, and ensure the smooth and rapid development of an integrated EU market. Formal intergovernmental bodies deal with these issues at the level of the EU. The dilemma for the island of Ireland is that the very specific harmonization needs of the North with the South may be imperfectly represented at present at the Brussels tables by the UK and Irish Governments, and Northern Ireland has no separate seat. The need to justify formal policy coordination bodies for the island of Ireland is not only an economic issue (as discussed earlier); it is also a political issue, since governments, or at least public sector agencies or utilities, have to engage in the actual planning and resolution of cross-border policy conflicts.

Under coordinated development, there is no reason to believe that the existing subvention financing of the North would be called into question. Indeed, this option would appear so attractive as a means of copper-fastening peace that a wide range of direct and indirect benefits could flow to the North, with beneficial spill overs to the South: US and EU direct aid; islandwide initiatives in the area of industrial promotion; cross-border initiatives to bring the border counties into the economic mainstream; a rethink of island regional policy; the evolution of an enlarged and more demanding domestic market to encourage greater innovation by indigenous industry. There can be few limits to where cooperation might lead, and ultimately the economic fragmentation of this island, however logical it may have appeared in the 1920s, might be reversed, as a single island economy evolves under whatever political structures are freely chosen.

4.3.3 A SINGLE ISLAND ECONOMY

In our concept of a single island economy, we envisage a situation of increased policy cooperation, over an appropriate time scale, leading to a virtually complete harmonization of economic and social policies and institutions, where it is found that their absence imposes costs on the island. No exact analogue of this scenario exists elsewhere, although useful insights can be obtained from the Benelux experience, suitably modified for the Irish situation.

Britain's constitutional and political position under this scenario could take many different forms. A politically minimalist form of the single island economy could conceivably take place within a post EMU federal Europe, where Europe wide convergence of a wide range of fiscal, monetary, industrial and other policies would act in support of the geographical proximity of North and South within such a Europe. An intermediate political form of the single island economy could come about as a result of devolution of economic policy-making powers to the North, while the North remains constitutionally part of the UK.[16] A politically maximalist form of the single island economy would arise in the case of a confederal, federal or united Ireland.

Clearly, our notion of a single island economy goes far beyond that raised by Sir George Quigley in his CII address (Quigley 1992). We are driven to deepen the concept because of our doubts that even the more restricted 'economic' concept of North-South cooperation could come about without the kind of political movement whose logic would require and facilitate an ever-increasing level of economic policy harmonization, leading eventually to a single island economy.

It is a fact that the present level of East-West economic interaction between the two individual Northern and Southern economies and the rest of the world (including

Britain in particular) is massively bigger than the present or any conceivable future level of interaction between North and South. However, the logic of intensive North-South economic interaction that would eventually lead to a single island economy is quite consistent with the importance of world markets as destinations for island of Ireland exports and the importance of external multinationals as sources of inward direct investment. The single island market would have its main economic benefits in deepening the supply-side links between producers on the island, in facilitating the growth of dynamic island firms that would use the integrated island market to develop and test new products, and ensuring a suitable environment for the eventual emergence of dynamic export-oriented island-based multinationals.

It is reasonable to ask how far a process of close policy coordination or harmonization is needed to ensure deepening of supply-side links between North and South. Also, does this call for cross-border institutions with effective influence and powers? Here the parallels with the development of the Single European Market and the process of evolution towards Economic and Monetary Union are compelling and have been discussed above in the context of policy coordination. An island economy is no more likely to develop in Ireland through the spontaneous actions of the private sector than the Single European Market would have developed in the absence of the Delors initiative in the mid 1980s (Cecchini 1988; Emerson et al. 1988). The rapid growth of intra-firm trade and cooperation within the EU, a development that is at the heart of faster economic growth, needed EU-level formal institutional arrangements. The lessons for the island of Ireland should be obvious.

In the light of the present acrimonious debate on European integration taking place in Britain, it is doubtful if the above logic of Irish policy integration will find complete favour. But it is not difficult to show that the present policy integration within the UK is not without its problems for the Northern economy. A considerable part of Northern industrial policy is aimed at offsetting the comparative advantage of the South, arising mainly from the ability to set a low rate of corporation tax, and compensating for the greater Northern peripherality within the United Kingdom, with subsidies that are often higher than their British counterparts. Research has shown that blanket, subsidy-based Northern industrial policies are very inefficient and generate big dead-weight losses (Sheehan 1993).

The size of the Northern subvention is irrelevant to North-South relations in a situation of separate development (McGregor et al. 1995). However, the subvention is a major stumbling block to any moves towards island policy harmonization that would require a large degree of Northern policy autonomy. Hence, to explore the possibility that the North might one day wish to move towards a situation of greater fiscal autonomy than at present, it becomes relevant to examine how the subvention could be reduced to the level, say, of the present Southern exchequer borrowing requirement. The period over which this could happen would obviously be influenced by the state of the world economy and the nature of transitional aid.

Two differing perspectives on the likely duration of the need for Northern subvention finance can be distinguished in the literature. McNally (1995) suggests that the size and movements of the subvention result from a combination of structural and cyclical factors. Examples of structural factors would include political, economic and social needs that arise naturally within a sovereign nation or integrated economic and monetary union. The key cyclical factors tend to be associated with the timing of the business cycle, such as the Lawson boom of the late 1980s and the subsequent UK recession. As the total UK public sector borrowing requirement (PSBR) rose during the recession years of 1990-1994, so too did the size of the Northern subvention. McNally points out that as the UK recovery proceeds, both national and 'regional' PSBRs will decline in tandem. However, since there has been no published research on the decomposition of the Northern subvention into structural and business cycle components, and since the Northern subvention was already very large at the height of the Lawson boom (£1.8 billion, or about 18 per cent of Northern GDP for the year 1990), clearly there are underlying structural factors that also need to be addressed.

A Cadogan Group analysis purports to show, on the other hand, that the subvention is a permanent feature of the Northern economy (Cadogan Group 1992). However, a problem with this kind of static analysis is that it fails to take on board the point that an island political settlement might conceivably release major economic forces that could work towards the regeneration of private sector activity within the North, and permit North-South synergies to emerge as businesses benefited from a larger and better integrated market of five and a half million consumers.

Indeed, the immediate and positive response of the island business community to the ceasefires, particularly in the areas of tourism, cross-border trade, agriculture and food processing, may give a valuable insight into the likely much greater response to a permanent peace accompanied by a political settlement that would represent a full normalization of intra-Northern, North-South and Anglo-Irish relations (D'Arcy and Dickson 1995). The implicit Cadogan assumption that the North is never likely to return to a better balance between regional expenditure and taxation would appear to be a vote of no confidence in the peace process and in the future of the Northern economy. Whatever its likely validity, the Cadogan view serves to deflect attention from a full exploration of real economic issues and potentials both for Northern growth and for North-South cooperation.

Thus, the present size of the subvention may not be central to long-term economic mechanisms through which supply-side links between North and South could be deepened. Firstly, the subvention grew to its present size through three decades of violence that seriously diminished the performance of the Northern private sector. This situation will be systematically alleviated as peace endures, and the size of the subvention is likely to shrink systematically as a share of Northern gross domestic product (GDP). Second, most Northern public expenditure is oriented towards health, social welfare, education, etc., rather than towards policy domains that bear more directly on industrial development.

The presence of the subvention, however, is important to the political dynamic through which the North might evolve towards an increased policy-making autonomy that would be essential to the harmonization of policy on this island and the promotion of supply-side deepening. Such evolution will depend on British and Northern attitudes to a continuation of a situation where the relative size of the Northern public sector remains large by British standards, or to the desirability of the alternative, where the Northern economy restructures in order to grow the relative size of its private sector. Hence, an increase in Northern economic self-determination may be a necessary condition both for the growth of the Northern private sector and for greater North-South economic policy cooperation.

4.4 OTHER NORTH-SOUTH POLICY CONFIGURATIONS

Our three evolutionary island policy configurations all focus on the North-South axis and represent possible paths of economic policy development that would be consistent with a wide range of political and institutional arrangements. The real danger is that failure to create a stable acceptable political solution on the island could delay, or even prevent, the emergence of a better economic and business environment. It is likely that there will always be a chain of causation running from politics to better economics and business, no matter how dynamic and farseeing the private sector, North and South, is on its own. Political settlement will always be a necessary condition for the optimal economic evolution and development of the island, even if it is not a sufficient condition.

Other writers have looked at the North-South policy coordination problem in many different ways.[17] The recent Forum report on short-term benefits of peace (KPMG 1995) looks at two ways in which peace in the North might evolve. The 'ceasefire (CF) scenario' is simply a cessation of violence unaccompanied by any movement towards putting in place a political settlement. Transitional benefits arise in this scenario, but it is probably best regarded in our framework as an example of separate economic development, mainly because most of the economic consequences are focused on Northern restructuring after the run-down and reallocation of security expenditures. The 'peace and political agreement scenario' (PPA) factors a political settlement into the CF scenario, but gives no details of the settlement other than to characterize it in terms of lower economic risk premia and a consequential faster and more complete transition to normality.[18]

An interesting series of Northern scenarios is presented in the Northern Ireland Growth Challenge and has relevance for the KPMG scenarios (NIGC 1995). We reproduce these in Figure 4.1 below.

Moving from scenario 1 (status quo) to scenario 4 (rebirth of enterprise) brings about different peaceful outcomes in terms of growth and decline. An interesting distinction is made between the slow decline envisaged under 'status quo' and the rapid decline under 'peace alone'. This highlights the crucial requirement for new policies to promote growth to offset the transitional negative shock that a simple run-down of government spending would impart to the North. Whether those policies come purely from the private sector or are a combination of private sector initiative and a complete rethink of public sector policy will mean the difference between stagnation and self-sustaining growth. We will return to these issues in chapter 6 below.

Scenario Dimension of change	Scenario 1 'Status Quo'	Scenario 2 'Peace Alone'	Scenario 3 'Private Sector Alone'	Scenario 4 'Rebirth of Enterprise'
FIGURE 4.1: NORTHERN IRELAND GROWTH CHALLENGE SCENARIOS FOR NORTHERN IRELAND'S FUTURE				
Insular/Conservative Culture	Continues	Continues	Succeeded by a new enterprise culture	Succeeded by a new enterprise culture
Social/Political Instability	Continues	Ends for a time	Ends	Ends
Expectations	Not met	Not met	Partially met	Met
Government Role	Supply-side fixes	Supply-side fixes	Supply-side fixes	Catalyst for change: market-driven support to competitiveness
Government Expenditure	Continues at present level	Falls quickly	Falls quickly	Falls after 4-5 years
Education and training	No change	No change	Little change	Produces knowledge assets ready for today and tomorrow
Capital influx from EU	One-off input for social benefit	One-off input for social benefit	One-off input for social benefit	One-off input for social and economic benefit
Outcome	Slow decline	Rapid decline	No growth	Self-sustaining growth

The DKM study of integrated North-South policy planning is an example of a range of reports that focus very largely on the public finance aspects of new North-South political configurations. O'Leary, et al. (1993) is a recent sophisticated update. As exercises in the public finance implications of ex ante constitutional configurations, such studies are helpful. However, they tell us little or nothing about how the real economies in such conceptualized States might perform.

5 THE WIDER SOCIO-ECONOMIC CONTEXT FOR THE ISLAND

5.1 INTRODUCTION

Public policy tends to be reactive rather than proactive in the economies of small countries or regions mainly because their scope for operating autonomous fiscal, monetary and industrial policies is heavily circumscribed. Such countries cannot spend their way to greater prosperity for several reasons (Armstrong and Taylor 1993, 305-328). Since their economies are usually very open, the expansionary effects of any increase in local expenditure tend to leak away into other regions. Since they are often in a weak financial position, they are restricted in their ability to raise the necessary finance for a substantial expansion of regional spending, in the case of sovereign countries, and run the risk of being caught in a dependency trap, in the case of regions.[1]

What unites small economies and sets them apart from large and powerful industrial economies is the premise of their economic policies, namely adaptation to external market and other forces. Small economies have generally found comprehensive or detailed sectoral planning methods to be inflexible and inappropriate to their problems simply because of their openness and consequential exposure to unforeseen and random shocks.

There remain two major roles for public policy in small open economies. First, policy can be used to improve the productive side of the economy, initiating activities such as infrastructural improvement, support for public education and training, and redistribution of income in a way that enhances efficiency, etc. Debates on economic policy during the last three decades have tended to focus on the optimum balance that should be struck between State intervention in the above areas and free market forces.[2] Second, public policy can play a role in facilitating adjustment to external and domestic forces that are beyond local control, where market failures and imperfections might otherwise lead to costly transitional disruptions.[3] Examples of external forces that are important to the island of Ireland include international developments in the areas of new technology and industrial organization. Long-term domestic forces mainly concern the island's demographics.

In this chapter we examine three strategic issues that will almost certainly condition future island growth under any of the three evolutionary North-South policy configurations discussed in chapter 4. Indeed, the manner in which domestic policy on this island reacts to these strategic issues will be at the core of the island's economic success or failure.

The first issue we explore concerns enterprise and industrial organization, where there is widespread recognition of the centrality of the manufacturing sector and the fact that past Irish performance in this area has left much to be desired. The North has suffered from a serious problem of deindustrialization that is part of a wider British pattern of decline, other than in centralized core areas near London and the rest of the south of England. Problems in the South (of Ireland) concern mainly the weakness of the indigenous sector and the unsatisfactory overdependence on inward foreign direct investment. Although there is much in common between recent trends in Northern and Southern industrial policy reform, there has been little or no formal attempt at policy coordination.

Our second theme concerns geographical and sectoral organization of the island economy, an issue that we have seen was relevant to the manner in which the island developed in the nineteenth century and to how it came to be politically partitioned in the early twentieth century. Recent trends in international specialization and the phenomenal success of other high-growth regions hold out great potential for the two economies of the island of Ireland. Prominent among such regions are Emilia-Romagna in Italy, Baden-Wurttemberg in Germany, Jutland in Denmark, Silicon Valley and Route 128 in the US, and the M4 Corridor in the UK. However, successful emulation by Ireland of such rapid growth regions is likely to need appropriate supporting domestic policies and a resolution of North-South and Anglo-Irish political issues. As we shall show, work in this area of policy design is still at a very preliminary stage, although recent Northern and Southern industrial policy reports have begun to draw similar lessons from the new literature of industrial organization (Stationery Office 1992; NIGC 1995).

The third theme we examine relates to human issues, such as demographic trends, human capital and wider labour market institutions. We saw that anomalous Irish demographic behaviour was central to the Great Famine and its aftermath, and endured well into the second half of this century. However, there have been recent demographic developments of a more benign kind that hold out some prospects of moving the two Irish regions towards the European demographic mainstream, thus easing some of the upward pressures on unemployment and outward pressures on emigration. Pressures on the public finances, North and South, would also be eased in the medium term, although in the long term one would expect an ageing population to generate increased expenditure on health, pensions, etc., similar to the present patterns in Germany.

Each of the above three issues raises concerns and has implications specific to the North and South separately, so understandably debate on them is carried out internally within each region. However, we wish to focus mainly on the context of North-South policy interaction in this report, so we highlight North-South cooperative aspects in our review.

Groups in both parts of the island unfortunately appear to be addressing the enterprise and industrial organization aspects in almost complete isolation,[4] even if some public and private sector organizations are collaborating on aspects of cross-border trade.[5] The second issue (spatial economics on the island) has arisen in the context of a private sector initiative in the guise of the Belfast-Dublin (or East Coast) Economic Corridor (Quigley 1992; Coopers & Lybrand/Indecon 1994), but has generated little or no North-South public sector policy response or engagement beyond a common chapter in the Structural Fund proposals of both regions (Northern Ireland Office 1994; Stationery Office, 1993). Concerning the third issue, considerable separate Northern and Southern research has been carried out in the area of demographic projections, but there has been little on other aspects of human capital and labour market institutions.[6]

5.2   ENTERPRISE AND INDUSTRIAL DEVELOPMENT

Discussions of industrial policy, North and South, have begun to take account of how the environment within which firms operate has been changing rapidly, with important consequences for the growth of successful clusters of modern innovative firms (Porter 1990; Best 1990). In the words of Michael Best, 'Industrial policy has no chance of success unless it is anchored by an understanding of the underlying principles of production and business organization.' Best's term for these processes is 'the new competition' (Best 1990). Michael Porter's framework of analysis focuses on the wider determinants of 'competitive advantage' (Porter 1990).

During most of the Industrial Revolution the geographical 'region' was a natural unit of economic activity and analysis. The nation's economy was simply the sum of its parts and national economic development was only marginally controlled by central political authorities. The growth of Belfast during the second half of the nineteenth century was a good example of such a semi-autonomous process (Bardon 1982). However, by the 1960s regions had become much less important as a focus of economic activity. According to Charles Sabel (1989), the demise of the old regional economies came about because: 'A system of mass production incorporated as subcontractors the pieces of the older regional economies which it had not already swept aside.' Present day industrial policy, both North and South, could be very crudely characterized as a process whereby national and regional agencies (the IDA in the South and the IDB in the North), using a wide range of incentives, bid for subcontracting roles from global multinational firms, and then attempt to influence the allocation of these activities over their respective regions in order to satisfy conflicting mixtures of economic, social and political criteria. However, the very success of inward investment to this island, in the South more so than the North, has tended to conceal the rapid changes that are taking place in the international market place, many of which have served to return the focus of attention to regions as natural units of production. Sabel (1989) lists the crucial developments as follows:

1. The emergence of conspicuously successful geographical regions, such as Silicon Valley and Route 128 in the US, the 'Third Italy', the 'Second Denmark', Baden-Wurttemberg, etc;

2. The dramatic reorganization of large multinational firms into many operating units with enhanced local autonomy;

3. The convergence of large- and small-firm structures: the former splitting up into specialized units; the latter grouping around centralized facilities (laboratories, marketing agencies, etc.);

4. The transformation of local governments from welfare dispensaries to job-creation agencies;

5. The cooperation of trade unions in the industrial reorganization at the plant or regional levels.

These changes have created a new form of local development that parallels emerging corporate patterns of behaviour (Sabel 1989). Like firms, the localities know that they must survive in a turbulent economic environment. Like firms, they must accommodate volatility through flexibility. For localities, flexibility requires facilitating the recombination of resources among companies, so that the latter may redeploy them internally. And as with firms, many localities will renovate themselves only with the greatest difficulty.

Empirical measures of international competitiveness are central to the attractiveness of regions like the island of Ireland. Such measures range from wage costs, output prices, profitability rates, etc., to wider measures related to product innovation, design, quality and reliability. Public policy can be invoked to influence an otherwise poor competitiveness position. The most extreme forms of intervention consist of import quotas and/or tariffs, methods used in the South during the protectionist period from the 1930s to the early 1960s. The preferred approach in recent decades is through subsidies to labour, capital, energy, etc., combined with lower rates of corporate taxation. Indeed, a striking similarity between North and South is the vigour with which State intervention is directed to enhance an otherwise average to mediocre level of international cost competitiveness, mainly through low corporate taxation in the South and high (though recently declining) subsidy rates in the North.

A cost-benefit study of factor subsidies and tax policy in enhancing competitiveness is a complex project in its own right. Recent analysis tends to show that while the effective exchequer costs of the Northern and Southern incentive packages are quite similar (NIEC 1995), the South's tax-based measures may be more efficient in economic terms (i.e., have lower 'dead-weight') than the Northern subsidy-based measures.[7]

Wider approaches, however, to defining and measuring the concept of national competitive advantage are desirable, that go beyond narrow, cost-based measures that economists find so tractable. For this, one needs to turn to Michael Porter's treatment of competitive advantage, a body of work that has been extremely influential in the recent reformulations of Northern and Southern industrial strategies (Porter 1990; Stationery Office 1992; NIGC 1995).

Porter asks how a nation can achieve international success in any particular industry or in groups of industries. His answers identify four broad attributes (the competitiveness 'diamond') that shape the environment in which national firms compete:

1. *Factor conditions:* the availability and quality of the factors of production such as skilled labour, infrastructure etc.

2. *Demand conditions:* the nature of local and external demand for the industry's product or service, where local demand can play a vital role in encouraging product innovation and improvement.

3. *Related and supporting industries:* the presence or absence of supplier industries and related industries that are also internationally competitive.

4. *Firm strategy, structure, and rivalry:* the national conditions governing how companies are created, organized, and managed.

Porter's main contribution to deepening our understanding of competitive advantage lies in the emphasis he places on the interactions between these four attributes and the detailed study of individual successful nations, regions and industries that illustrate these interactions at work. This approach has been used to great advantage by the South's Industrial Policy Review Group, or Culliton Report, (Stationery Office 1992) and more recently by the Northern Ireland Growth Challenge (NIGC 1995a).[8] However, it has been applied to North and South in isolation from each other, and ignores synergies and spill overs that might arise in the context of the wider economy of the island of Ireland. Nor has it been applied to large cross-border regions like the Belfast-Dublin Economic Corridor area, or to smaller sub-regions like Newry-Dundalk and Derry-Letterkenny, areas where local analysis has a tendency to become divorced and isolated from national trends.

It seems very likely that both North and South have quite low scores on all of the components of the Porter diamond, except perhaps for factor conditions.[9] How might this situation be improved? Both regions are individually small, with populations of 1.6 and 3.6 million respectively. Northern Ireland is not only separated geographically from Britain, but also appears to be very weakly integrated into the supply side of the British economy, even when demand for Northern output is dominated by the British market. For example, the North is not central to strategic planning by British firms in the sense that the Southern market is central to, say, Munster-based firms. How many British-based firms have their corporate headquarters in Northern Ireland? How many firms with a dominant position in the UK market have their origins in the North?[10] Northern Ireland appears to be not only geographically peripheral to Britain, but is also economically peripheral.

This lack of supply-side integration with Britain is due in part to the problems created by the past twenty five years of the troubles. Recent improvements in access transport (e.g., super ferries) and the stability that peace will bring, will probably alleviate this situation over time, but is unlikely to ever place the North on a par with the rest of the British economy (at least from the supply-side perspective). Rather, it is likely to remain the case that the North will always be somewhat economically peripheral to Britain, but there is less logic to the North remaining economically peripheral to the South.

The logic in favour of deepening North-South supply-side links, thus making the two Irish regions less peripheral to each other, is partly economic (dealing with cross-border policy externalities and spill overs), partly geographic (close proximity and land borders have a unique and inescapable logic of their own), partly cultural (although this aspect is not without problems), and partly political (since deeper North-South economic links might aid the consolidation of peace between the different Northern communities and greater trust and harmony between North and South).[11]

The situation in the South relative to the countries that provide the bulk of Southern foreign direct investment (i.e., the US, Britain and the rest of the EU) has strong analogues with the position in the North. For example, the Southern economy is not central to the strategic planning of US-based firms, other than as a highly profitable location for production of products mainly designed, developed and tested elsewhere, and a location where a very high quality labour force is available. The branch plant nature of foreign firms located in the South tends not to encourage the building of strong performance on the Porter diamond. Dependence purely on external investment is unlikely to generate the type of cumulative self-sustaining growth that is a characteristic of the successful growth poles listed above.[12]

Hence, it may prove beneficial to consider ways in which North-South coordination could lead to improvements in Irish scores on the Porter diamond. These could include enhanced demand conditions (arising from the stimulation to product innovation provided by the larger island market); growth of related and supporting industries (arising from clustering associated with North-South inter-firm linkages); and strengthening of firm structure and inter-firm rivalry (associated with a more competitive island business environment). We take up these issues in the next chapter when we examine possible growth scenarios for the island economy.

At present both North and South are attempting to improve their competitive advantages according to the Porter diamond in isolation from each other. Given the political climate of the last few decades, this process of separate development is easy to understand, since the type of public and private sector planning and consultation needed to build a Porter-type strategy would have demanded levels of cooperation that were never going to be politically feasible during the troubles. However, this situation is changing rapidly, mainly under pressure from the private sectors of North and South, through organizations like the CBI in the North and IBEC in the South.

The planning and coordination needs of pursuing a strategy of improved competitive advantage requires close cooperation between the private and public sectors through government agencies, employers' organizations and trades unions. In the South this process has become well established and works reasonably well (O'Donnell 1995). However, to a Southern economist it would appear that the situation in the North is not working as smoothly, and the recent NIGC initiative would appear to point up, however subliminally, problems with existing policy-making structures.[13]

5.3 SPATIAL ISSUES: INFRASTRUCTURE, CLUSTERS AND REGIONAL DEVELOPMENT

5.3.1 GROWTH CENTRES AND CORRIDORS

Geographically concentrated growth centres and corridors have three defining features:

- Economic activity tends not to be spread uniformly over space or over sectors, but tends to cluster or concentrate;

- Such clustering is clear evidence of some kind of increasing returns (i.e., doubling inputs more than doubles outputs) and this should be exploited by policy-makers;

- Growth centres in specific locations (usually cities of above a certain size) will tend to interact with each other over space to form corridors, or elongated growth centres.

As a description of the dynamics of growth the above points have wide application. The first element simply describes the physical realities of the cities, towns, villages and less populated hinterlands to be found in any country or region. The second element provides an economic explanation for why clustering occurs, and has been a very active area of research in industrial economics over the past decade (i.e., the 'new' growth and trade theories). The third element is a logical consequence of the first two and merely describes the interaction of two or more contiguous growth poles as their areas of influence begin to overlap. Corridor development must, of necessity, lag behind the first two, since growth poles must exist and prosper before they can fruitfully interact. In the absence of vibrant growth poles there can be no corridor.

5.3.2 SOME PRE-1960 IRISH EXPERIENCE

In his treatment of inter-war Southern industrialization Ó Gráda (1994) comments:

> Industrial policy during the protectionist 1930s, when much of Southern indigenous industry was set up, was better geared towards generating employment throughout the country in the short run than towards building up a self-supporting Irish industrial sector. The preoccupation with regional dispersion reflects this. Practically every town was promised its own factory or factories, ruling out scale economies and external

95

economies, and virtually guaranteeing that the new plants would be parochial in their ambitions. (P. 398.)

An example given was the Drogheda-based shoemakers, Woodingtons, who, in the 1930s, were forced by civil servants to locate their tannery in Gorey, County Wexford, rather than adjacent to their existing factory. This was typical of the hothouse growth of small plants reliant on a protected home market. It ensured that the natural growth of inter-firm cooperation, within given local specializations, would never happen, and that such firms as existed would be unlikely to survive when tariff barriers were dismantled in the 1960s.

Inter-firm cooperation and industrial 'districts' failed to develop in the protectionist South, from the 1930s to the 1950s, largely as a result of an industrial policy that minimized the likelihood of geographic clustering in a not very successful effort to spread employment more evenly throughout the regions. It is not surprising that the resulting weak indigenous sector performed so poorly when faced with stiff international competition in the 1960s after tariff barriers were lowered. In the long run, the regions were poorly served by such a policy of dispersal, however beneficial were the short-term gains.

We have already seen that the situation in the North was very different. Here, the size of crucial sectors such as shipbuilding (Belfast) and linen (Dungannon-Newry-Belfast) ensured the existence of considerable scale economies. The extraordinary success of the north-east region, centred on Belfast, meant that this was the only Irish region that fully participated in the latter stages of Britain's industrial revolution, becoming what economists refer to technically as an 'industrial district'. The spill over benefits from the Belfast growth pole were felt throughout the north-east region, and by 1911 the population of Belfast had outstripped that of Dublin.

After partition, however, Belfast's problem became one of stagnant or declining world demand for its main products, combined with a failure to restructure into newer product areas. The negative effects on towns such as Newry were serious, as the growth pole process went into reverse.[14] By the 1950s much of Northern indigenous industry suffered from many of the problems of its Southern counterpart: dispersal, small size and inward orientation.

5.3.3 POST-1960 SOUTHERN EXPERIENCE

While the north-east growth pole centred on Belfast had arisen in an era of *laissez faire*, the debate on concentration versus dispersal in both the North and the South was revived in the 1950s and 1960s in the context of *public policy* initiatives designed to tilt the balance predominantly in one direction or another. The Buchanan Report of 1968 was a comprehensive statement of the key issues for the South. The Matthew Report of 1963 was an earlier statement of issues in the North. The subsequent public debate, North and South, is illuminating and decisions taken in the early 1970s still largely shape both economies, as well as conditioning present day attitudes to regional policy on the island.

The first suggestion of a switch to a more spatially selective industrial policy in the South appeared in 1958 in *Economic Development*, the background document from which the First Programme for Economic Expansion drew its inspiration. The debate on growth centres versus dispersal flourished during the early to mid-1960s, culminating with the commissioning of the Buchanan Report in 1966. After extensive review of past performance and analysis of options, Buchanan proposed a new policy orientation that embodied the growth centre idea, namely that 75 per cent of new industrial employment over a twenty year period should be concentrated into a limited number of urban areas (Figure 5.1). In particular, the development of two national growth centres at Cork and Limerick would enable them to attain a sufficient size to compete effectively with Dublin. In addition, six regional growth centres and four local centres were to receive preferential treatment.

As might be expected, these proposals generated a vigorous and sometimes acrimonious debate. The Government was reluctant to implement them, opting essentially for a continuation of the previous policy of dispersal. The formal rejection of the policy of concentration was eventually embodied in the first five-year plan of the Industrial Development Authority (IDA), published in 1972, and formal growth centre policy was quietly dropped.

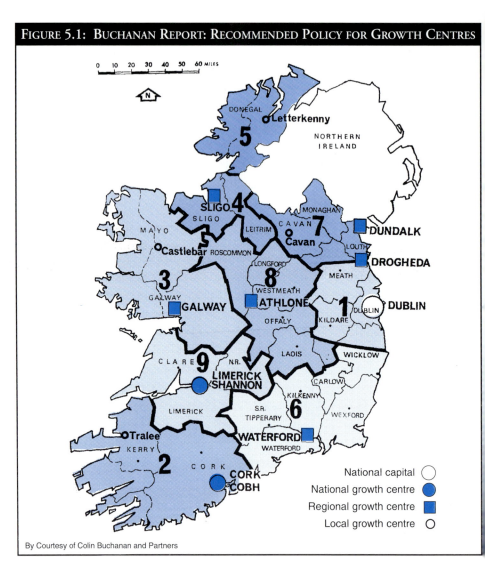

FIGURE 5.1: BUCHANAN REPORT: RECOMMENDED POLICY FOR GROWTH CENTRES

By Courtesy of Colin Buchanan and Partners

A major economic argument against the promotion of growth poles made by the IDA was that improvements in transport and communications had greatly increased the locational flexibility of industry and that this was reflected in the ability of the weaker regions, outside the proposed Buchanan growth centres, to attract and support foreign direct investment. IDA policy was formulated in terms of systematic regional dispersal, accompanied by a comprehensive programme of fully serviced industrial sites and advance factories and greater locational variability in grants made available.

To the extent that IDA policy was indeed targeted at a redistribution of manufacturing employment more evenly throughout the country, it was quite successful. Figure 5.2(A) shows *location ratios* for 1961, where these are obtained by dividing the percentage of total employment in manufacturing by the percentage of the total population. A value of unity indicates employment shares that are exactly proportional to regional population. Figure 5.2(B) shows the position in 1991. In fact, by the late 1970s the earlier obvious bias in favour of Dublin (the east region) had been largely removed and all the other regions had improved their position. By 1992 some regional heterogeneity was creeping back, although the shift of jobs from manufacturing to market services probably distorts the 1992 figures.[15]

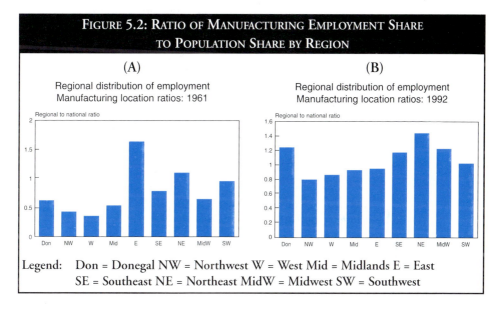

FIGURE 5.2: RATIO OF MANUFACTURING EMPLOYMENT SHARE TO POPULATION SHARE BY REGION

(A)

Regional distribution of employment
Manufacturing location ratios: 1961

(B)

Regional distribution of employment
Manufacturing location ratios: 1992

Legend: Don = Donegal NW = Northwest W = West Mid = Midlands E = East
SE = Southeast NE = Northeast MidW = Midwest SW = Southwest

The success in dispersing new manufacturing employment to the regions, illustrated clearly in these graphs, was accompanied by a more modest, but nevertheless significant, convergence in regional per capita incomes in the South. Indeed, greater convergence of regional incomes might have resulted if the policy of decentralization of public sector services out of Dublin had been pursued more vigorously.

Such an equitable regional outcome might suggest that concentration was not necessary to ensure both strong national and regional growth. However, a different, less benign interpretation can be made based on specific features of the Southern experience of foreign direct investment, which was the main source of post-1960 industrial growth. Rereading Buchanan today with hindsight forces one to reconsider his rather unsettling questions in the context of subsequent developments. Commenting on past policies, Buchanan had asked:

> But has this success in terms of regional distribution been won at high cost? Would a greater degree of concentration in location of industry have resulted in the new enterprises doing better, in existing enterprises doing better, and in the rate at which new enterprises are set up being accelerated?

The foreign-owned industries locating in the South were originally, and largely remained, branch plants that seldom became involved in the core stages of product design and development, these activities remaining with the foreign parent company. Instead they were involved in relatively routine assembly and manufacturing processes, often at the standardized stage of the product cycle. However, branch plants are better than no plants. All nations start by importing their technology, and the most common way to do this is to encourage foreign direct investment and to train the labour force in the servicing of this investment, simultaneously working to try to increase the level of indigenous competence.

If it could be shown that these branch plants, against a background of spatial dispersal, began to interact with each other, gradually took on increasingly complex tasks, and moved towards the earlier stages of the product cycle (i.e., 'maturing' products or, eventually, 'new' products), then the growth centre idea would really be in trouble. The Irish evidence here is difficult to interpret and to do so would be a major research project in its own right. International commentators tend to be more optimistic than domestic analysts. For example, Castells and Hall (1994) in their analysis of 'technopoles' comment that:

> New countries and regions emerge as successful locales of the new wave of innovation and investment, sometimes emerging from deep agricultural torpor, sometimes in idyllic corners of the world that acquire sudden dynamism. Thus, Silicon Valley and Orange County in California; ... Silicon Glen in Scotland; the electronics agglomeration in Ireland; ... .

One interpretation of the Southern experience could be that, far from being a late-comer, the South, after executing an extraordinary policy volte face in the 1960s, was among the early countries to benefit from the production, transportation and communication advances that first generated internationally mobile investment flows on a large scale in the late 1950s.[16] With an early start, a comprehensive range of incentives and a high level of human capital, the IDA succeeded in attracting an impressive share of this investment. Since these branch plants required little in the way of interaction with the local economy, they could be dispersed among different regions.

While the policy of dispersal had little effect on multinational branch plants, which were relatively self-sufficient and sourced only a small fraction of their inputs in Ireland (and only a tiny fraction locally), any anticipated synergies between foreign firms and between foreign and indigenous firms, were probably very seriously impeded.[17] Once again Buchanan's comments on the earlier period of industrialization, if somewhat overstated today, come back to haunt us:

> Almost nowhere have [enterprises] been sufficiently large and flourishing to trigger off a secondary development of other enterprises, for example to supply components, undertake further processing or provide specialist services. Government grants have, at best, produced the scheduled number of new industrial jobs — they have not set off a self-sustaining cumulative growth process which will build up strongly in years to come without further injections of support from outside.

Given the complexities of the Irish industrialization process, it is difficult to make an absolutely convincing case that the policy of dispersion of multinational branch plants definitely did impede the development of synergies between foreign and indigenous firms. However, there are many direct and indirect indications that what synergies did come about were at best weak. For example, although industrial output and exports grew rapidly in the key areas where foreign-owned multinational firms dominated (e.g., chemicals, pharmaceuticals, computers, instrument engineering), the employment response was very attenuated both in these key sectors themselves and in the industrial and service sectors that would be expected to benefit from synergies (NESC 1992). Furthermore, IDA work on targeting foreign-indigenous synergies (e.g., the

National Linkage Programme) is designed to strengthen what are admitted to be weak linkages.

Geographic dispersion was obviously not the only issue at the root of the problem of weak foreign-indigenous synergies.[18] In addition, the gulf that existed between the new high technology foreign-owned firms and existing largely traditional indigenous industries was probably too large to bridge satisfactorily during the first decades of the export-led growth strategy. However, although the inter-firm synergies may have been weak, there were obvious direct benefits to the Southern economy in terms of conventional income multiplier effects. A further important benefit came through human capital and labour market externalities, as the expansion of the Southern education system after the mid-1960s interacted with the demand of the foreign sector for an increasingly skilled labour force. After three decades of large-scale inward investment, the position in the South is now transformed, and we return to the new potentialities in chapter 6 below.

5.3.4 POST-1960 NORTHERN EXPERIENCE

Policy on sub-regional development and industrial location within the North was relatively weak and passive from the immediate post war period until the mid-1960s, tending to accommodate development in the north-east sub-region. As late as 1962 the Hall report on the economy of Northern Ireland devoted little attention to regional imbalances or to the active use of public policy to redress these imbalances, even in light of the serious unemployment in areas west of the Bann, such as Derry, Enniskillen and Strabane, and in Newry and Dungannon to the south of Belfast (Hall 1962).

However, the *Belfast Regional Survey and Plan* (the 'Matthew' Report) was the first of a series of reports that began to focus on sub-regional imbalances (Matthew 1963). Unlike the South, where physical planning tended to follow behind economic planning, economic plans for the North up to the mid-1970s accepted the essentials of the physical strategy as put forward in the Matthew Report. In Figure 5.3 we illustrate the 'growth' and 'key' centres as designated by Matthew, where the concentration on the eastern sub-region is apparent.

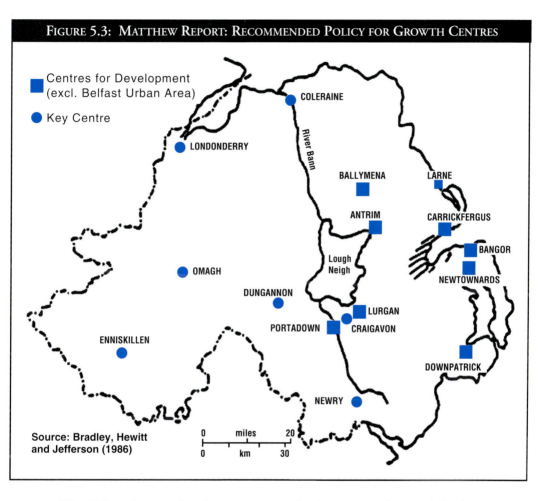

FIGURE 5.3: MATTHEW REPORT: RECOMMENDED POLICY FOR GROWTH CENTRES

The Wilson Report of 1963 on economic development in the North further promoted the concept of growth centres, and worked on the assumption that successful regional development would be accompanied by internal migration: people moving to jobs, rather than jobs moving to people. However, correcting a previous anomaly, Derry was designated as a growth centre.

A major change in regional policy was heralded by the Quigley Report of 1976. An acknowledgement of the segmentation of Northern labour markets and the relatively low rate of internal migration led the review team to the conclusion that:

103

It is simply a fact that no regional policy (whatever its success in promoting investment or raising GDP or reducing unemployment) will be judged satisfactory which fails to remove the unemployment black spots. (P. 17.)[19]

From the mid-1970s, it could be said that regional policies in both North and South eschewed any narrow focus on growth centres and became a pragmatic blend of concentration and dispersal that attempted to bring spatial equity to the island, with as little loss of economic efficiency as possible. Indeed, Southern research indicated that the failure rate of firms in the underdeveloped regions and smaller towns had been no higher than in the large urban areas, and firm formation rates appear to have been reasonably evenly spread over all Southern regions.[20] This suggests that the policy of branch plant dispersal did not entail a large sacrifice in terms of employment (Brunt 1988).

A final aspect of the Northern sub-regional policy debate concerns its implications for, and impact on, the spatial distribution of Government-sponsored employment in relation to the religious composition of the population. Contrasting with the scattered nature of the Catholic majority areas, the non-Catholic community forms a reasonably solid contiguous group in the east-central region of Northern Ireland. Consequently, any economic policy that facilitated further concentration on the east-central region, either passively or actively, could not avoid the relative neglect of the large areas with Catholic majorities. Figure 5.4 shows manufacturing 'location' ratios for the entire period 1949-1981, together with two sub-periods: the passive policy period 1949-63, and the active policy period, 1964-81.[21]

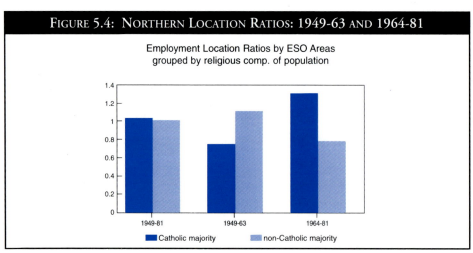

FIGURE 5.4: NORTHERN LOCATION RATIOS: 1949-63 AND 1964-81

Employment Location Ratios by ESO Areas grouped by religious comp. of population

Although there is no overall difference for the entire period, there is a marked difference between the two sub-periods, with Catholic majority areas faring better during the later 'active' policy period than during the earlier 'passive' period. One is left to speculate that had the situation been reversed, and had the relatively deprived areas with Catholic majorities benefited more in both employment and housing during the first period rather than the second, then perhaps at least some of the underlying causes of the outbreak of civil unrest in the late 1960s might have been alleviated.

5.3.5 SUMMARY

Our brief examination of the previous and the present stance of industrial policy, both North and South, suggests that the normal processes of clustering and regional concentration eventually were impeded both by the branch-plant nature of the investment and by a public policy of geographical dispersal. The only example of an Irish self-sustaining 'industrial district', i.e., Belfast during the period from the mid-nineteenth century to the early decades of the twentieth, declined thereafter. More recent policy has deliberately promoted regional dispersal, almost certainly at some expense to strict economic efficiency criteria.

After more than three decades of exposure to foreign direct investment, however, the South has succeeded in attracting sufficient firms in the computer, instrument engineering, pharmaceutical and chemical sectors to merit a description of sectoral 'agglomerations' or 'clusters'.[22] The incentives used in the South to attract and hold these firms were tax breaks, grants and a well educated and trained work-force. With the exception of tax-based incentives, similar policies were used in the North to attract inward investment, albeit in a climate dominated by negative factors associated with the troubles.

We have seen that the Northern Ireland Growth Challenge draws attention to the successful clusters or agglomerations in certain Southern industrial sectors. It is obviously of interest to Northern policy-makers to explore ways in which these Southern processes could be broadened to include the North, having regard to the nature, needs and characteristics of these sectors. This raises a host of policy and industrial organization issues that go to the core of any quest for islandwide synergies and we take them up in chapter 6. However, we examine one aspect now, since the idea of strengthening the economic corridor linking the cities of Dublin and Belfast has been the subject of public discussion (Quigley 1992) and a recent major consultancy report (Coopers & Lybrand/Indecon 1994).

5.3.6 COULD THE EAST COAST BECOME A DYNAMIC ECONOMIC CORRIDOR?

Sir George Quigley's initial ideas on the possibility for an economic corridor to link the city economies of Belfast and Dublin, were taken up in an IBEC/CBI(NI) commissioned feasibility study (Coopers & Lybrand/Indecon 1994). This study had three main objectives: to explore what lessons could be learned from international experience of growth corridors; to establish the feasibility of developing a corridor along the densely populated east coast of the island; and to investigate the impact such a corridor would have on the rest of the island economy.

We have seen above that the growth centre idea is a very powerful one, growth centres are seen to exist in practice, and they can be explained in terms of various types of agglomeration economies. However, given that a policy of dispersal of manufacturing activity has been pursued in both the North and South for at least the last two decades, it is unlikely that detailed examination of the present state of industrial activity in the corridor area will produce strong evidence in favour of growth centres or, a fortiori, strong patterns of interaction between the Belfast and Dublin poles. Since the Southern policy of dispersal seems to have achieved many of its rather limited economic and social aims, would a reversal of policy in favour of concentration be equally or more successful? Looking at the issue in another way, to what extent are international examples of successful corridors the result of autonomous forces or policy induced? How might such policies be framed in the case of Belfast-Dublin or elsewhere on the island?

In the first part of the corridor feasibility study, a range of international corridor experience is surveyed. All twelve cases examined were in large, wealthy countries, with high standards of living. All have very sophisticated transport infrastructure that serves to define and support the corridors. They are corridor success stories, whether through historical chance or conscious planning. We learn little from them of cases of failure of other adjacent urban areas to link into highly dynamic and productive corridors.

The study then extracts common features of the successful corridors and these can be classified into three main headings:

1. The fundamental requirement of a high standard of physical infrastructure;

2. Good support facilities (i.e., government agencies, university linkages, support services, availability of venture capital, etc.);

3. An appropriate sectoral structure and orientation of production (i.e., interaction between companies, export orientation, tourism and amenities).

Not surprisingly, the feasibiliy study found that successful corridors have good infrastructure and excellent support facilities, are home to clusters of dynamic, mutually interacting, export oriented manufacturing firms supported by a sophisticated service sector, and, what is more, are nice places in which to live and socialize. Their success breeds further success, and they illustrate the operation of virtuous circles.

In order to explore the extent to which the Belfast-Dublin economic axis replicates, or could come to replicate, the conditions for a successful corridor, the second part of the IBEC/CBI(NI) feasibility study consists of a socio-economic review of the corridor area, consisting of six Southern counties (Dublin, Kildare, Meath, Cavan, Monaghan and Louth) and three travel-to-work areas (TWAs) in Northern Ireland (Belfast, Craigavon and Newry). This comprises just under 20 per cent of the island land area and contains 50 per cent of the island population.

Besides being a useful survey in itself, and pointing to some obvious features of the corridor area (such as a population and educational establishment concentration on the cities of Dublin and Belfast and a lower than national average employment in agriculture), it is interesting to see that the corridor profile is in many ways not very different from the aggregate national profile. All things considered, the island of Ireland comes across as a rather spatially homogeneous place, other than in terms of the special concentration of population around the cities of Dublin and Belfast.

Since a central feature of successful corridors lies in the superior performance of manufacturing industry, the third part of the study turns to an analysis of the performance of industry in the Belfast-Dublin corridor area. If there are to be distinguishing features of the corridor area we would expect to find them here. However, since the data used are mainly from the Census of Industrial Production (CIP) and the IDA Irish Economy Expenditure Surveys (for the South) and Census of Employment (for the North), one can only describe industrial characteristics, such as employment and output performance, in a very aggregate way.

Even so, the data illustrate once again the homogeneity of patterns of industrialization on the island. Such homogeneity might be expected for the South, in light of the analysis of the policy of dispersal discussed above. It is a little surprising for the North, given the predominant role played by Belfast in nineteenth century industrialization, and the history of concentration found up to the early 1970s. Hence, rather than showing that the corridor area displays economies of agglomeration, and that Belfast and Dublin are growth poles, what emerges is a picture of constant returns to scale and economic homogeneity against a background of spatial population concentration.

In order to examine the detailed way firms in the corridor interact, or fail to interact, with each other, we need information on individual firms, and this is not easily available. We need to know why they located in the corridor rather than elsewhere; if the presence of other specific industries, services or facilities was central to that decision. Surveys were taken by Coopers & Lybrand/Indecon of just under 400 individual firms, and the information gathered is of some limited use. What information there is paints a very gloomy picture of the poor sub-supply linkages between the Northern and Southern parts of the corridor. In effect, the sub-supply linkages are 'trapped' by the strong pull of the two large urban centres at each end of the corridor, the explanation for which may be partly political, but is probably mainly historical-economic.

The feasibility study then provides an analysis of the spatial distribution of the largest seventy five firms (measured by employment) along the corridor and examines clustering of a range of seven manufacturing sub-sectors. What emerges is a dominant pattern of concentration near the two cities at opposite ends of the corridor, with a scatter of relatively isolated firms in between. However, little is said about the deeper, non-spatial, aspects of clustering as examined, for example, by Michael Porter, who asserts that nations succeed not in isolated industries, but in *clusters* of industries connected through vertical and horizontal relationships.

We know practically nothing about how the firms in the corridor interact with each other. Since published data are largely unavailable, neither do we know whether smaller firms are closely integrated with the larger ones in the corridor. Also, since no picture is given in the report of the wider island economic-spatial situation, we do not know if the corridor clustering is significantly different from that occurring around other Irish cities like Cork, Limerick, Galway or Derry. Basically, we do not know whether the corridor is just the geographical place where these plants happen to be located, or whether it is a synergistic and innovative milieu; whether there are constant or increasing returns. However, some negative responses to the Dundalk RTC survey of company attitudes in the Newry-Dundalk area to formalized inter-company cooperation tend to point towards relatively isolated firms who have few opportunities to share information, and are often unwilling to do so (RDC 1994).

The questions that arise as one attempts to move from the present weak economic linkages in the corridor area to a more dynamic situation where the benefits of intra-corridor synergies are realized, take one to the core of North-South policy cooperation and will require the creation of an islandwide business environment that will be more conducive to growth. The failure of the corridor area to develop such synergies in the past can be explained in many ways, some of which are specific to policy choices made within the North and the South (intra-regional factors). Additional explanations concern the failure of inter-regional cooperation. Both explanations are of relevance as we contemplate the future, and we take up these issues in chapter 6.

5.3.7 EXAMPLES OF CROSS-BORDER REGIONAL COOPERATION

A major legacy of the unhappy history of this island has been that the normal social and commercial intercourse one would have expected to develop and flourish between two adjoining regions became stunted. This process of separate development was particularly damaging to the cross-border region, which suffered a double level of peripherality within the partitioned island. We single out two examples where recent developments have attempted to address some of the problems of the border area and repair the damage of the legacy of separate development: the North-West Cross-Border Group — a mainly local authority initiative — and the efforts that are being made to revive the local cross-border economy in the Newry-Dundalk area — mainly a business-driven initiative.

The North-West Region Cross-Border Group

The creation of the border was both an economic and social disaster for the isolated north-west region of the island. The Southern counties of Donegal, Leitrim and Cavan were cut off from their hinterlands in the Northern counties of Derry, Tyrone and Fermanagh and the organic growth of the region, with a focus on Derry, its largest city, was seriously inhibited. Early informal cooperative efforts between Donegal County Council, Derry City Council and Strabane District Council go back to the period just after Irish and UK entry into the EEC. This resulted in the publication of a *Donegal/Derry Communication Study* in 1977, highlighting the communication needs essential to the development of the region, commissioned by the Irish and UK Governments, with EC aid. Further work was carried out on priorities for public investment in the area, involving liaison between the local authorities, the national Governments and EC officials. However, little came of these early initiatives other than the experience of working together across the border, forging deeper links and collaborating in the routine business of local government.

The concept of integrated local development was encouraged by the European Commission during the mid-1980s as a means of increasing the impact of Community and of national funding in peripheral areas suffering severe economic disadvantage. This provided a logical focus for the Cross-Border Group's activities but their efforts were ultimately unsuccessful in obtaining specific funding resources. In 1985 further new initiatives in the area of tourism were proposed, embracing four council areas and involving Bord Fáilte and North-West Tourism in the South and the Northern Ireland Tourist Board and Foyle Tourism in the North, but once again failed to secure adequate funding.

In the late 1980s the process of cross-border cooperation shifted into a higher gear with the commissioning of the North-West Study, jointly funded by the British and Irish Governments and the EC. This involved an in-depth survey of the economy of the north-west region and a series of detailed recommendations on policies to stimulate growth in this relatively deprived area. The launch of the study by the then Taoiseach, Charles Haughey and the Northern Ireland Secretary of State, Peter Brooke, gave a renewed impetus and focus to the group's cooperation and to the joint lobbying of EC Regional Policy Commissioner Bruce Millan. An immediate concern was to place the existing ad hoc organization on a more formal basis. Of the eleven applications made by the group under INTERREG I, one was successful and permitted the setting up of a full-time secretariat in 1992 and the appointment of a development officer based in offices located in Derry.

The North West-Region Cross-Border Group functions as a committee of the four councils (Donegal, Derry, Strabane and Limavady), made up of eighteen of their elected representatives (six from Donegal and four each from the Northern Councils), together with the four CEOs. The monthly meetings alternate between the four council venues, with a rotating Chair. Given its local government origins, the group is concerned primarily with public sector initiatives but acts as a focus for a far wider and more diverse set of public and private sector initiatives in the region. For example, a recent group project spearheaded by Derry involves the preparation of a directory of public and private services in the region and a brochure to attract inward investment.

A major conference was organized by the group in November 1993 (Highlight North-West: Shaping the Future Together), at which a wide variety of public and private sector activities were presented. These ranged from European local government cooperation; an overview of experience with INTERREG I; a live video link with Commissioner Bruce Millan; a presentation of the activities of the International Fund for Ireland; a review of ERNACT, a European network of local authorities for the implementation of communications technology; a presentation on ECOM, a European Economic Interest Group consisting of European Chambers of Commerce; presentations by some private firms in the communications technology area; and discussion of cross-border tourism initiatives.

In November 1994 the group published its new development programme in anticipation of INTERREG II. In it a range of local and cross-border development themes are identified in areas such as indigenous enterprise, tourism, access infrastructure, public and private services, and rural development, with specific projects described and costed. Of particular interest is the move to have a small subset of the overall development plan funded by a global grant and implemented by the Cross-Border Group as an integrated programme. Such a proposal would bring some of the key decision making into the north-west region area and give the group real resources to address local issues in an fully integrated and cooperative way. Here, the north-west region is giving a lead in building on the opportunities that peace will provide and helping to restore the cross-border links that were so damaged by history and by the troubles.

The Newry-Dundalk Initiatives

We refer to the region that embraces the Newry-Mourne District Council area and an area of some 15 miles radius centred on Dundalk, as Newry-Dundalk, although no

111

such region yet exists in any policy-meaningful sense. The characteristics that make this region unique come from the close proximity within it of the two largest towns along the Belfast-Dublin axis; the history of industrial growth and decline in these two towns, that is almost certainly associated in large part with the border between them as well as with the weakness of the two city economies at the corridor's extremities; the fact that neither town has overcome this impediment to growth, and both now have rates of urban unemployment that are among the highest on the island.

Research carried out subsequent to the IBEC/CBI(NI) corridor feasibility study has initiated the taking of an inventory of the local Newry-Dundalk economy, *The Newry Business Opportunity*, prepared by Enterprise Newry and the first report of the Cross-Border Technology and Innovation Project, prepared by Dundalk RTC. The task faced by the researchers in developing a picture of the Newry-Dundalk area is made difficult by the lack of good regional data sources and further complicated by the existence of a 'data' border, that prevents the uniform conceptualization of the economy of a region that straddles the North-South border. Nevertheless, from the data that are available, a picture emerges along the following general lines:

- A static population for the whole Newry-Dundalk area, with growth in the North (Newry and Mourne), but population decline in the South (Dundalk);

- A present rate of unemployment that is significantly higher than the national averages (but similar in the North and South of the area if adjustment is made for Government schemes), together with very serious unemployment black spots in particular local areas;

- Good local educational infrastructure and a particularly high rate of second and third level education in the Northern labour force, though combined with a sizeable fraction who have no formal qualifications.

- A pattern of sectoral employment that is heavily weighted towards services (including public services) in the North of the area (72 per cent of Northern employment) and more weighted towards manufacturing in the South (32 per cent of Southern employment), although the mixture of rural and urban areas in the North makes such a comparison difficult.

- A manufacturing sector that is heavily weighted towards small and very small firms, that probably service local rather than export markets.

- No obvious pattern to the structure of the manufacturing sector, which probably represents a mixture of indigenous firms who managed to secure niche markets and a regional 'share' of foreign industries, who located for national cost and incentive reasons rather than for local sub-supply possibilities.

Even though the above is a summary of the far from optimistic economic and social situation of the Newry-Dundalk region, there are recent developments that hold out possibilities of radical transformation. Funding for local initiatives is now available from a range of different sources: the International Fund for Ireland; the EU INTERREG programme, now in its second phase; and the recent EU Fund for Peace and Reconciliation, much of which will be directed at the Northern and Southern border counties. Public sector organizations and private firms in Newry and Dundalk have deepened the scope of their cross-border cooperation. The high-technology business incubation unit based in the Regional Development Centre of Dundalk RTC is pioneering such cooperation, in conjunction with similar Newry-based organizations. Joint proposals on food technology and scientific parks are also being drawn up on a cross-border basis.

The urgent need for economic regeneration in the Newry-Dundalk area suggests that one should examine what Bernard Share has recently referred to as 'the only example of sustained and effective regional endeavour in the country in modern times', namely the Shannon region (Share 1992). This is a region which is differentiated from any other in the South in that its commercial, industrial, social, educational, tourism and urban development has been or is currently the responsibility of a specific state-sponsored body, SFADCo. The conflicts between the regional development body (SFADCo) and the national industrial promotion agency (IDA) are well documented in Share's history of the Shannon regional initiatives, and pose the dilemma of how to reconcile a desire for regional autonomy with national priorities in a small island like Ireland.

It will be necessary to examine whether Newry-Dundalk, for example, has sufficiently well-defined characteristics and potentialities to sustain a regional development initiative along the SFADCo lines. The split in jurisdiction caused by the border will undoubtedly complicate policy cooperation within any such region, an aspect that was absent from the SFADCo area. The previous policy of separate Northern and Southern development has not served the Newry-Dundalk area well, and since the cross-border region is where the negative aspects of policy mismatch are greatest, the challenges of overcoming the associated problems will be considerable.

Given the comparatively weak powers assigned to local government, North and South, it is doubtful if the deployment of measures required for the regeneration of the area could operate purely at the local level. However, any moves towards policy cooperation at the national level, or towards a single island economy, will have immediate effects on the manner and scope of cross-border economic regeneration, bringing these regions back into the economic mainstream of the island. The SFADCo analogue only becomes relevant in a situation of North-South policy cooperation, or, a fortiori, in the context of a single island economy.

The fact that both towns are broadly in the 'catchment' areas of their adjacent large cities could be a hindrance if this works to prevent an emerging regional identity that Limerick/Shannon obviously enjoys. Nevertheless, if regional growth in the Newry-Dundalk cross-border area were to prove elusive, the whole concept of the larger East-Coast Economic Corridor would be seriously called into question. An obvious danger is that both Dublin and Belfast will function as isolated growth poles, with only weak spill overs into the intervening regions (the fear of a Belfast-Dublin 'tunnel' rather than a 'corridor'!). Success in regenerating the Newry-Dundalk region could prevent that happening.

5.4 HUMAN ISSUES: DEMOGRAPHY, HUMAN CAPITAL AND LABOUR MARKETS

5.4.1 THE UNEMPLOYMENT PROBLEM

Failure in the labour market is a shared characteristic of North and South. Not only has the North long had the highest rate of unemployment among the regions of the UK (Figure 5.5), but the South has had one of the highest rates in the European Union, exceeded only by Spain and briefly by Finland after the collapse of the Soviet Union (Figure 5.6).[23] Southern research has shown that being unemployed is the single most important factor in explaining the incidence of poverty, and that long-term unemployment is at the centre of mechanisms explaining the transmission of deprivation to following generations (Callan et al. 1989; Breen et al. 1990).

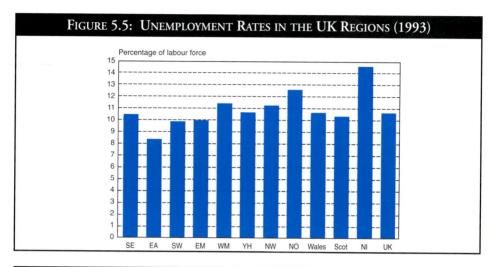

FIGURE 5.5: UNEMPLOYMENT RATES IN THE UK REGIONS (1993)

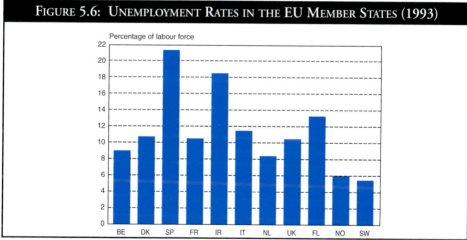

FIGURE 5.6: UNEMPLOYMENT RATES IN THE EU MEMBER STATES (1993)

A further complication in the Northern case is the differential that exists between unemployment rates when broken down by religious affiliation. Research shows that the average rate of unemployment among Catholics is over twice the average rate among the other denominations (Murphy and Armstrong 1994). The investigation of the causes of this phenomenon has generated vigorous disputes in the Northern literature.[24]

5.4.2 FUTURE IRISH DEMOGRAPHICS

While the natural growth of population in the South exceeded the European average there was strong upward pressure on labour force growth. In a situation of slowly growing demand for labour, this tended to exacerbate both the level of unemployment and put pressure on outward migration. However, the position changed dramatically in the early 1980s, when the birth rate fell from a level of about twenty two per thousand to the present level of about fourteen, and is expected to decline further (FitzGerald 1995).

The decline in the birth rate is likely to result in very dramatic changes in one of the key factors that have been keeping the Southern unemployment rate high. For example, assuming zero net migration, labour demand must grow by at least 20,000 per annum if the present rate of unemployment is to be maintained. By the turn of the century this will have fallen to 15,000 and by 2006 to below 10,000. In addition to removing pressure on the growth of the supply of labour, there will be beneficial implications in the medium term for many other areas of public expenditure and an opportunity to improve quality of service delivery within a fixed budget, although the long-term effects may be less uniformly positive as the population ages (the 'grey' effects).

The situation in the North is less clear. In his analysis of Northern population projections, Compton (1995) suggests that the interaction of a falling birth rate with resumed outward migration will cause the Northern population to peak in 2011 and decline thereafter. In other aspects, both North and South share many demographic trends and their labour market implications. This is an obvious area where joint North-South research would be useful and the recent paper by Ó Gráda and Walsh (1995) examines the demographics of the island.

5.4.3 HUMAN RESOURCES AND GROWTH

An overview of past Northern and Southern public expenditure in the area of education and training has been provided in Bradley, O'Donnell and Sheridan (1995). In addition, the stock of educational qualifications, education participation rates and types of qualifications are compared, North and South.

The current situation in both regions is one where a high proportion of the total work force has only very basic education, although new entrants to the workforce tend to have considerably higher qualifications than older workers.

This is likely to cause problems of low competitiveness and productivity, but also means that an upgrading of skills among the current workforce can only be achieved at the margin, in terms of new entrants. This has particularly important implications for the North, where projected increases in foreign direct investment are set to increase demand for highly educated and trained labour.

Low levels of vocational qualifications exist in both regions, a feature that may be the result of both a low demand and scarcity of supply. Demand and supply aspects will need to be involved in treating the problem. In 1992, the Culliton Report asserted that the Southern educational system was excessively academic and called for a dual system of general and vocational education operating in parallel (Stationery Office 1992). The Green Paper on education of the same year rejected this call, but proposed to expand provision of vocational education and technical subjects within the senior cycle of second level schools. The results of Breen and Whelan (1995) would seem to indicate that the latter approach is more consistent with the nature of the Irish labour market, North and South, and the fact that the business sector is weakly collectively organized. A recent analysis of educational policy in the North, *Learning for Life*, proposes to encourage greater vocational attainment by incorporating additional subjects in the post age sixteen curriculum.

The large numbers of unemployed in both economies require retraining and second chance education if they are to have any chance of competing effectively in the labour markets. The flow of unqualified school leavers from the education systems needs to be stemmed before they too are added to the numbers of the long-term unemployed. Many sectors of industry and services could reap considerable benefits from a more intensive use of better qualified school leavers and graduates, but traditional businesses seem reluctant to do so. These are some of the main challenges facing the education systems of North and South.

The relationship between human capital and economic growth is very complex. A closely related issue concerns who benefits from human capital accumulation: the private individual and/or society at large? A positive relationship is observed at the individual level between human capital accumulation and earnings, and this is usually taken as evidence of increased productivity. Since the 1960s, economists have explored whether or not there exists an externality associated with education, training and learning-by-doing.

The *private* return to education, as considered by economists, is defined as the extra benefit which accrues to the individual as a result of undertaking increased education and/or training. The *social* return includes the private return, the increased income in the economy which results from greater consumption and investment by the educated and trained, and the economy-wide increase in output which results from the presence of externalities. In the presence of outward migration, however, the domestic social return can turn negative, even if the private return remains strongly positive.

As the numbers of unemployed have increased, a dual labour market has tended to develop. The long-term unemployed have ceased to play an active role due to skill obsolescence, reduced motivation and search effort and poor employer perceptions. Competition for jobs in the rest of the labour market has intensified and resulted in higher levels of qualifications being demanded for all jobs. People are often employed in jobs for which they are over-qualified and which do not utilize their skills and knowledge to the full. The education and training accumulated by these individuals is under-utilized and so neither the individuals concerned nor the economy reaps the full return of the human capital accumulation.

Research into the effectiveness of training and employment schemes in Ireland has been limited. O'Connell and Lyons (1994), in a preliminary analysis of a subset of cases from a follow-up survey of adult participants in such schemes, argue that post-scheme placement rates in employment are not adequate performance indicators because they take no account of participants' background characteristics — such as age, sex, educational qualifications and prior labour market experience — which they found to strongly influence post-programme outcomes. Similar results were found by Breen (1991), who analysed the effectiveness of training and temporary employment schemes in the youth labour market and concluded that significant positive effects of training and temporary employment schemes existed in the short term but that there were no significant long-term effects for either scheme.

One must be careful not to paint too gloomy a picture of the state of education and training in the two regions of Ireland. There are now high average educational participation rates in the South, and a high proportion of high attainers in the North compared with the rest of the UK, and an OECD report showed the high attainment rate of tertiary education in the South (OECD 1993). Indeed, foreign investors in both regions frequently cite the young, highly qualified work force as an attractive incentive to investment.

5.4.4 LABOUR MARKET STRUCTURES, NORTH AND SOUTH

An underlying factor in the different economic performances of North and South lies in the institutional set-up of industrial relations and wider issues in the two labour markets. Teague and McCartney (1995) describe the different situations that pertain in the two Irish regions in relation to wage structures, training systems and skill formation, dispute resolution mechanisms and human resource management.

Two main conclusions are drawn by Teague and McCartney. First, there seems to be little need for any large-scale programme to bring labour markets, North and South, closer together in the short to medium term. It is suggested that their differences may not be of major importance, and that there are likely to be few economies of scale in all-island labour market programmes. Second, the economic and institutional conditions are not in place to sustain any attempt at full labour market harmonization in the short to medium term, even if such a goal were felt to be desirable. The complex interdependencies that give rise to national labour market structures could place severe constraints on cross-border collaboration. In the long term, given suitable political and economic cross-border institutions, the island may need to evolve towards a more integrated labour market, a process that would be greatly facilitated if the UK participated more in EU labour market policy-making.[25]

In particular, it is possible to argue that an island-scale labour market may provide a superior context for developing and retaining more highly qualified brainpower within the island. Crucial to the development of such a market would be the requirement to harmonize personal tax regimes, social welfare regimes, and a wide range of other health, education and social policies that have a bearing on the efficient operation of the labour market. Hence, Teague and McCartney, by focusing mainly on the institutional and training aspects of the labour market, may have understated the wider economic and social benefits of an integrated labour market in an island economy.

PART III
FUTURE DEVELOPMENT PLANS

6 THE TWO ISLAND ECONOMIES: FUTURE DEVELOPMENT PATHS

In the previous two chapters we have examined some of the public policy and wider external and domestic issues that will set the context for the future growth prospects of the two economies on this island. For ease of exposition we have tried to develop these two themes — domestic policy-making structures and other islandwide economic issues — in isolation from each other, although it should be obvious that they are always going to be closely interrelated in practice. We now try to put the two themes together and chart some of the economic development possibilities that may open up for the economies of North and South and the island economy over the coming decades.

Almost all decisions made by policy-makers in government and business are based on a view of the future and for policies dealing with new opportunities and potentials for this island a particularly long-term view may be necessary. To undertake such a task we need to identify some of the likely key influences on Northern and Southern development over a time horizon of up to twenty years. This may seem presumptuous, but such long horizons are increasingly used in the European Commission and elsewhere to improve the strategic orientation of policy that must, of political necessity, be sometimes designed and usually implemented in a short- to medium-term time frame.[1] It should go without saying that such long-term scenarios can never play the role of forecasts. Rather, they are attempts to conceptualize possible future situations that could have major influences on the efficient management of the economy and on the orientation of present policy design.

Even in more normal Irish circumstances this would represent a daunting challenge. However, the possibility that peace in the North may facilitate a major reassessment and restructuring of the Northern economy over the next decades, and that North-South economic interactions may extend and deepen, makes this challenge even more daunting. If, as is the case, prospects for the Northern economy over the next twelve to eighteen months are difficult to predict with any degree of certainty, one might reasonably be sceptical about an analysis of prospects for the next decade or two. Hence, some explanation of our presumption is called for.

6.1 FORECASTING FUTURE ISLAND GROWTH

The conceptual backgrounds to short- and long-term economic forecasting are very different. In the short-term case one wishes to anticipate the immediate response of the economy to random domestic policy and external shocks that are likely to occur over, say, a time horizon of six months to two years at the most. The focus is on *cyclical* movements about the underlying trend of the economy rather than on the long-term determinants of the underlying trend itself. In the medium- to long-term case 'the focus shifts to the determinants of the underlying trend where now the cyclical movements about trend become more conjectural, although remaining of some interest. Quantitative forecasts beyond a five year time horizon can never be more than illustrative scenarios showing possible consequences of hypothetical assumptions and relatively unchanged structures and institutions. For even longer time horizons a qualitative exploration of issues tends to be more useful than a problematic quantitative projection. The material in this chapter is mainly of the long-term qualitative exploration type.

The ESRI *Quarterly Economic Commentary* uses a forecasting horizon of between twelve to eighteen months. The ESRI *Medium-Term Review* moves the detailed projection horizon out to five years (presently to 2000 in Cantillon et al. 1994). The nearest Northern equivalent is the medium-term forecast drawn up by the NIERC. This presently goes out to 2000 in Gudgin and O'Shea (1993), although it has recently been extended to 2004. These medium-term forecasts were prepared prior to the ceasefires and have not been formally updated to take into account the impacts of the ceasefires.[2]

It is of interest to note that the present ESRI medium-term GNP growth forecast for the South (averaging just under 5 per cent per annum) is over twice as high as the NIERC/OEF forecasts for the North (averaging about 2.3 per cent per annum), where this is already almost a doubling of the earlier Northern forecast contained in Gudgin and O'Shea (1993). What this means is that both North and South are reasonably likely to enjoy steady growth over the next few years, with low rates of emigration and declining, though still high, rates of unemployment. The higher growth projections for the South are associated with the dynamic performance of the high-technology sector, a sustained competitiveness in the rest of manufacturing, and continued stability and improvement in the public finances. For the North, the key forces driving the projected growth rates are less clear, but seem to depend mainly on the strength of the British economy in one way or another.

Since these forecasts, or revisions of them, form the starting point for any long-term analysis, it is important to understand possible threats to the forecast scenario of medium-term stable growth before we proceed to look at the long-term consequences of alternative North-South policy and business configurations. With one exception, the type of threats we have in mind have little or nothing to do with North-South interactions or Northern peace developments.

First, the economies of North and South are vulnerable to unanticipated crises in the world economy, since both are very open to external trade. We develop this point in more detail in section 6.2 below.

Second, a cornerstone of Southern performance over the past nine years has been a systematic improvement in cost competitiveness that was facilitated by a series of corporatist-type agreements negotiated between employers, trades unions and Government (O'Donnell 1995). These agreements underpinned Southern cost competitiveness by ensuring industrial peace and wage growth that was consistent with membership of the narrow band of the EMS. Clearly the South would be seriously exposed if expectations changed and the stability provided by the present corporatist-like arrangements broke down. The North, however, has had to forge an uneasy compromise between British-type free market policies, on the one hand, and more inclusive social partnership arrangements that perhaps accord more naturally with the situation of a small peripheral region.[3] The consequences of an unexpected outbreak of industrial unrest or of a wage-price spiral in Britain could be very serious for the North, where wage setting and industrial relations arrangements are still largely locked into British analogues.

A third issue of importance for North and South relates to the pattern of external financial subvention. We have dealt with the North in chapter 3, where the present British subvention amounts to over £3 billion per annum, making up some 30 to 40 per cent of public expenditure or some 20 per cent of Northern GDP. Clearly the future performance of the Northern economy would be very vulnerable if this subvention were to be reduced as a matter of policy by the British Treasury.[4] The South's annual subvention amounts to some 6.5 per cent of GNP and is made up of Structural Funds and price supports paid under the Common Agriculture Policy.[5] It is very unlikely that this level of support will be reduced before 1999, the termination year for the Delors II round of Structural Funds, or that major reductions in the CAP payments system are imminent. However, it is quite possible that reductions could be made early in the next century, with more of the available Structural Funds being directed perhaps towards the less advantaged regions in Greece and Portugal and to new applicants for EU membership in Central and Eastern Europe.

A fourth issue concerns European Economic and Monetary Union (EMU), and will be central to future island performance and to economic and business relationships within the island and between the island and Britain. If the United Kingdom and the South participate jointly in the scheduled evolution of EMU, then present British-Irish and North-South difficulties arising from differences in the areas of fiscal, monetary, enterprise, labour market and regional policy would tend to become less serious over time. However, should the UK choose to deviate from some elements of EMU, the South will be faced with policy choices that may, as an unintended consequence of its planned participation in EMU, disrupt North-South economic cooperation and damage growth.

The difficulties already caused for Southern trade with Britain by Britain's unpredictable relationship with the European Monetary System (EMS), and a fortiori for the subset of intra-island North-South trade, should alert us to wider problems that might flow from British approaches to a single European currency within EMU. Clearly, this will be an important area for consideration by Southern policy-makers in arriving at their decision about participation in EMU and about the safeguards that would be needed to protect the Southern economy against large-scale devaluations of sterling, should Britain stay out and attempt to operate an independent exchange rate policy.

Any exploration of the future performance of the island economy must be carried out against the background of simplifying assumptions in all four of the above areas. We summarize our assumptions briefly, and return to these matters later in the chapter. First, we assume that there will be no world economic crisis for the foreseeable future, in the full knowledge that the economies of both North and South would be extremely vulnerable to any such crisis, irrespective of whatever specific North-South policy configurations evolve over time. Second, we assume no sudden change in expectations concerning industrial relations and wage bargaining that would jeopardize the maintenance of competitiveness.

In the case of the third factor, we assume that the important but relatively modest level of EU subvention to the South is run down in a planned and orderly fashion after the turn of the century, with the Southern economy growing out of its previous Objective 1 status.[6] We return to this point in section 6.2 below. Any problems created by the much larger Northern subvention are the subject of specific assumptions in each of our three evolutionary North-South policy and growth scenarios. Finally, the issues involved with future EU developments, including Economic and Monetary Union, are extremely complex and are at the centre of political debate both within Britain and between Britain and other EU member State governments. These difficulties cannot be assumed away in any simple way and we take up some of the issues involved in the next section.

In the remainder of this section we first set out very briefly some of the features of the world economy that will influence the performance of the two Irish economies. These include world growth, changes in the pattern of world trade and industrial development, the broadening (or enlargement) of the European Union, and reform of the Common Agriculture Policy (CAP). We then look at possible future evolutionary paths for the two economies on the island. For each of the three island policy scenarios, outlined in chapter 4, we examine how the island economy might perform, how the different levels of North-South interactions and institutions are likely to influence this performance, and the type of policy and institutional change that would produce the best economic out-turn within given political constraints.

6.2 THE WORLD ECONOMY AND THE ISLAND OF IRELAND

Under this heading we include the opportunities and threats posed for the island of Ireland by developments in the world economy over the next two decades. Here we can only touch on the issues involved, which include:

World Economic Growth

Although both North and South have very open economies (in the sense that their export and import ratios to GDP are very large), they will not always respond symmetrically to shocks that emanate from outside the island of Ireland. First, any such shock that serves to increase world interest rates (such as German unification did in the early 1990s), will dent Southern performance more seriously than that of the North. The main factor here is that the level of public sector indebtedness in the South is considerably higher than the level in Britain.

Second, a purely British recession would normally be expected to have stronger influences on the North than on the South, simply because of the greater Northern trade and FDI dependence on Britain. However, the recession in the North in the early 1990s was considerably milder than in some of the core regions of Britain, mainly because of the protection from cyclical downturns afforded to the North by its large public sector and the continued British commitment to sustain a generous level of subvention finance. In the South, on the other hand, trade exposure to the British market is lower than for the North. Nevertheless, the Southern businesses exposed to the British market contain some of the more employment intensive and less competitive firms in the indigenous manufacturing and service sectors. This tends to magnify the influence of British recessions, as well as magnifying the benefits of booms in the British economy.

Changes in the Pattern of World Trade

The development of the Pacific Rim and the continued liberalization of world trade will present both opportunities and threats for this island. For example, the Northern (Ireland) textiles and clothing sector will face new challenges with increased competition from the rapidly growing economies of Asia. The multinational investment in the South (of Ireland) is already concentrated in high technology areas, and so is less vulnerable for the present. However, both North and South are likely to face greater competition for increased shares of mobile foreign direct investment. Since neither region could be classified as having low costs, there will be continued need to compete in terms of quality factor inputs, an aspect of the Porter diamond discussed in chapter 5 above.[7]

Patterns of Industrial Development

The Delors White Paper on Competitiveness and Employment identifies biotechnology and information technology as the emerging technologies which will fuel growth in the EU economies into the next century. Since this is a very rapidly evolving area, it will be necessary to examine the sectors which are likely to grow as a result of these technological developments, the current position of North and South in respect of these sectors, and the preconditions in terms of infrastructure and human capital investment for successful development in these sectors. Also of importance are the nature of agglomeration economies for these emerging sectors, the extent to which elements of these benefits can be shared in the context of foreign direct investment (in the absence of indigenous global players), and the implications for North-South cooperation between firms.

In today's world technological and economic progress are interdependent. By sharply reducing transportation and telecommunication costs, national economies are becoming increasingly interdependent and the whole globe is being brought into what US Labour Secretary Robert Reich (1993) refers to as 'the global network':

> The real economic challenge ... [to the nation] ... is to increase the potential value of what its citizens can add to the global economy, by enhancing their skills and capacities and by improving their means of linking those skills and capacities to the world market. (P. 8.)

This process of global competition is organized today mainly by multinational firms and not by governments. Production is now modularized, with individual modules spread across the globe so as to exploit the comparative advantages of different regions. Hence, individual small nations and regions have less power to influence their destinies than in previous periods of industrialization, other than by refocusing their economic policies on location factors, especially those which are relatively immobile between regions: the quality of labour, infrastructure and economic governance, and the efficient functioning of labour markets.

Broadening of the European Union

The European Union is now a community of fifteen. Over the next ten to fifteen years, a number of the transitional economies in Eastern Europe, such as Hungary, Poland, the Czech Republic, Slovakia, Slovenia, etc., are likely to join the Union. Thus, Ireland will become one of many small peripheral economies in the European Union. This will have implications in terms of core-periphery policy in the Union, in particular for the Common Agriculture Policy and the Objective 1 status of the island.

A consequence for the two regions of Ireland is that they are eventually likely to forfeit their classification as Objective 1 (or lagging) regions, and with it their high level of EU Structural Funds for development purposes. This is more serious for the South, which has not got the resources of Britain at its disposal. Hence, the use of the existing Delors II round of Structural Funds will be vital to the long-term improvement in Southern infrastructure since the opportunity may not recur in as generous a way in future rounds.

Recent statements by EU Regional Policy Commissioner Wulf-Mathies, however, suggest that financial aid flows to the island of Ireland and to the other 'cohesion' countries could remain significant after the completion of the 1994-99 CSF. The economies of the Visegrad countries, much less those of Bulgaria and Romania, are unlikely to be unable to absorb the amounts of EU funds that might be diverted from the present recipients towards the end of the present decade. Given the early stage and slow pace of their economic reforms, these potential EU applicant States may be unable to sustain Structural Fund-type programmes, since they could put unbearable strains on their fragile monetary situation, their limited financial capacity to absorb and co-finance such funds and administrative capacity to utilize such funds effectively.

Nevertheless, the loss of Objective 1 status, should it occur, is likely to have positive aspects that may well outweigh any diminution in the level of EU funding. Both regions of Ireland will enter the twenty first century with a much improved physical infrastructure and with a level of human capital in the labour force that will be second to none within the EU or the wider world. The ability of the South to fund a continued high level of public investment in infrastructure and human capital to a greater extent out of its own domestic tax and borrowing resources, will depend on translating the potential for faster sustained growth into reality. The North will be less affected, since under present constitutional arrangements it can always draw on the considerable resources of the British Government.

Reform of the Common Agriculture Policy (CAP)

Within the next decade the CAP is likely to undergo major changes. The driving forces for change will be the potential entry of Central European States, especially Poland, into the EU and the next round of world trade reform under the auspices of the World Trade Organization (WTO). Both factors will drive the EU towards separating income support from production aids (Kearney 1995). A number of studies suggest that once there is a complete decoupling of income support from production, the logical approach will be to transfer the cost of income support to national governments (Anderson et al. 1994; Folmer et al. 1995).

Whatever the pace of change in the CAP, it seems likely that farmers, both North and South, will see a fall in real output prices towards world market levels in the early years of the next decade. However, it has been suggested that because of its low-cost extensive production process, Irish agriculture could prove competitive in this changed environment (Boyle 1992). While a fall in prices would discourage production, other things being equal, the highly constrained nature of the agricultural sector means that, with the removal of quotas, output of certain products, especially milk, could actually increase. Any increase in the supply, at a lower price, of what is a raw material input for the food processing sector, could also help to improve competitiveness in that sector.

The future standard of living in the agricultural sector generally will depend on the speed with which these changes take place and the extent to which farmers' current favoured position within the EU budget is fully translated into direct income transfers as the price level falls. At present it seems likely that the income transfers will initially cover most of the loss which CAP reform could involve. However, in the very long run the generosity of this support could be eroded, especially if the income supports are nationalized. The relatively large numbers of farmers in the South (of Ireland) would make national funding of income supports expensive in the long run. The weaker political position of farmers in Britain could also leave farmers in the North vulnerable to a phasing out of income transfers in coming decades.

6.3 EVOLUTIONARY DEVELOPMENT PATHS

6.3.1 SEPARATE DEVELOPMENT

We have defined separate development as resembling the institutional and business situation that prevailed before the ceasefires with only modest North-South economic and business interaction and limited formal policy coordination between the Northern and Southern public authorities. It also represents the background against which existing ESRI and NIERC/OEF medium-term economic forecasts were prepared, where North and South can be treated in almost complete isolation without much loss of information (see above).

It should be stressed that the separate development scenario is being increasingly by-passed by rapidly evolving events on the ground. It is now, and is likely to remain, a scenario of yesterday rather than of today or tomorrow, provided the stimulus to North-South interaction associated with the ceasefires continues to gain momentum. However, we consider it a relevant starting point for a few reasons. First, it serves as a useful way of conceptualizing the economic and policy status quo ante. Second, many aspects of a previously very limited North-South interaction still endure. Third, the view that there may be very significant economic benefits for the island arising out of an increased level of policy and business cooperation is not universally accepted. Hence, the separate development scenario is the minimal case that can serve as a benchmark for evaluating evolutionary alternatives.

If indeed North and South were to continue on a path of separate development, their long-term growth performances could deviate from each other, mirroring differences in underlying driving forces. For example, the key driving forces in the South will relate to its continued ability to capture a share of high quality foreign direct investment and to build on the benefits of its existing embryonic agglomerations in key sectors such as computers and software, food processing, health technologies and international financial services. Furthermore, recent changes in Southern demographic patterns, with a much slower projected growth in population and labour supply from the turn of the century onwards, hold out the prospects for a systematic reduction in the Southern rate of unemployment over the medium to long term, together with a steady improvement in the quality of public services in areas such as education and health.

Under a scenario of separate development the North would continue to behave as a region of the United Kingdom. Hence, although peace will bring about an increase in foreign investment from the US and elsewhere, the North would probably maintain its heavy dependence on the British economy as the major source of its external direct investment, as the main market for its products, and for sustained support from the British exchequer if Northern public expenditure continues to exceed Northern tax revenue. Opinions as to the future dynamism of the British economy differ. However, some commentators suggest that Britain runs risks of growing more slowly than the core EU economies, the US and Japan, due to its low level of investment in physical capital, infrastructure and education and the dominant role of a financial sector that is inimical to policies designed to support long-term growth (Hutton 1994).[8] The problem for the North is that there is a danger it may suffer the fate of being a slow-growing region within a slow-growing nation.[9]

We already know a good deal about the likely consequences of the peace process for the immediate future. Since existing policy structures and institutions are slow to change, particularly in a period of political uncertainty, the category 'separate development' may be the appropriate stylized one to use for short-term analysis. Private sector business initiatives, however, are forcing the pace of North-South interaction, but must do so mainly in the context of the existing national policies.

For example, background assumptions made in the calculations presented by KPMG in their analysis of the short-term economic consequences of the peace are consistent with a mixture of separate and coordinated development scenarios.[10] The crucial effects concerning the run-down of security spending and its reallocation to other areas of the public and private sectors, are mainly of concern to the internal management of the Northern economy, within existing policy institutions, although they are not entirely without spill over impacts on the South (KPMG 1995, 39-56). Other beneficial effects associated with inward investment and tourism operate against a background of business cooperation and involve a certain element of public policy coordination (KPMG 1995, 23-34).

The main KPMG results, in terms of their employment effects, are illustrated in Figure 6.1 below. Four aspects need to be highlighted:

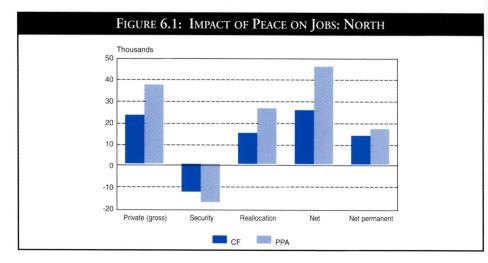

FIGURE 6.1: IMPACT OF PEACE ON JOBS: NORTH

1. Both peace scenarios (CF and PPA) generate substantial employment gains in private sector activities such as foreign industry locating in the North, tourism, increased cross-border trade and indigenous industry (see Figure 6.2(A)). The modest Southern gains are associated with growth in a range of market services (including tourism), indigenous industry, public expenditure savings and agriculture);[11]

2. Substantial job losses are associated with the reduction in the size of the Northern security forces;

3. , If the public expenditure savings that result from the reduction in the security forces are 'recycled' into essentially public employment projects, then a net increase in public employment would result if the cost of each job created is assumed to be much less than the cost of the average security job lost;

4. Employment increases in the private sector are classified into those that are permanent (i.e., would be sustained even in the absence of public subvention) and those that are temporary (i.e., would vanish if the public subvention were to be discontinued).

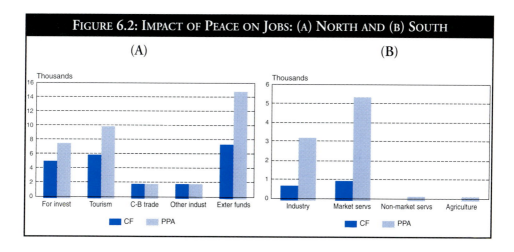

FIGURE 6.2: IMPACT OF PEACE ON JOBS: (A) NORTH AND (B) SOUTH

The total net gains North and South, before reallocation of Northern security-related savings to mainly public sector job creation elsewhere in the North, are illustrated in Figure 6.3, where the mid-range estimates have been taken as representative of the likely out-turn.

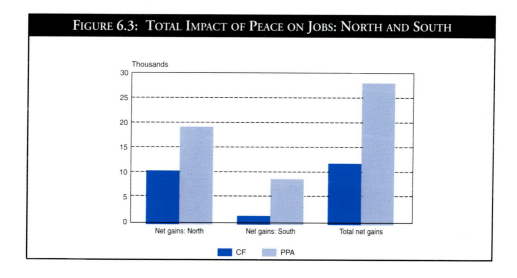

FIGURE 6.3: TOTAL IMPACT OF PEACE ON JOBS: NORTH AND SOUTH

The crucial issue in evaluating long-term economic consequences of the KPMG analysis of the peace dividend is to ask whether that dividend will bring about a *one-off* transitional change in the level of activity, or whether it holds out prospects of launching both North and South on a path of sustained faster *growth*. Were the scenario of separate development to resemble the situation envisaged by the Northern Ireland Growth Challenge in its 'rebirth of enterprise' scenario, then there might be some hope in bringing about a sustained shift upwards in the Northern growth rate. In the South, the measures proposed by the Industrial Policy Review Group (in the Culliton Report) are designed to increase growth.

However, the Northern business sector and policy-makers may experience considerable difficulty in implementing an economic planning process that would lead to 'a rebirth of enterprise' in a situation where they continued to be locked into British policy norms. At the same time we have suggested in the previous chapter that the Northern economy is only imperfectly integrated into the supply-side of the much larger British economy. In terms of British economic links, this appears to be the worst of all possible situations for the North. If, in addition, the North remains unlinked to the somewhat larger Southern economy, it may lack the critical size to facilitate and sustain a purely Northern virtuous circle of growth.[12]

The KPMG report draws attention to another possible gain for North and South that could conceivably be initiated under the separate development scenario, namely gains from increased cross-border trade. Here there is considerable conflict between the very optimistic calculations of the CII (now IBEC) and a more pessimistic analysis of the NIERC (CII 1990; Scott and O'Reilly 1992). The key points at issue are set out in Table 6.1.

Since the economies of these islands (i.e., Britain, the North and the South) are quite closely interrelated through trade in goods and services and labour flows, in Figure 6.4 we compare and contrast sales of Northern and Southern produced manufactured goods per capita of population in the market served, for the two Irish regions and Britain. Figure 6.4 shows that home sales of Southern goods per capita exceed home sales of Northern goods per capita by a factor of almost two. Furthermore, sales of Southern goods in the North, per capita of the Northern population, are about three times the value of sales of Northern goods in the South, per capita of the South's population. The direction of the excess is easy to rationalize in terms of the larger size of the Southern economy and the trade deficit that the North presently runs with the South (see chapter 3). However, the actual magnitudes are a little surprising and indicate scope for future growth of Northern penetration of the Southern market.

Table 6.1: Could there be a North-South Trade Bonanza?

Combined sales by manufacturers North and South within the island of Ireland market are about £6 billion (in 1990). The CII claimed that there is a potential to increase this to £9 billion, thereby creating 75,000 new jobs (CII 1990). The claim is based on the following three assumptions:

A. Northern manufacturers could sell as much in the South, in per capita terms, as they presently sell in their domestic market. A similar assumption is made about Southern sales in the North.

B. All these increased sales displace imports from outside the island, rather than from other Irish producers.

C. Every extra job created in manufacturing induces an extra 1.3 jobs in the rest of the economy, i.e., the employment multiplier is 2.3.

Scott and O'Reilly (1992) reject assumption A and argue that the existing level of sales between the two regions of Ireland appears to be in line with the level of sales between other small European countries and their nearest neighbours (e.g., Denmark's sales in Sweden). Furthermore, sales by the North are £110 per head of Southern population, compared with £37 per head in Britain.

They regard assumption B as being very optimistic, particularly if sales displace the goods of the other region (e.g., food products). A more realistic target might be to double cross-border trade from £1 billion to £2 billion, and with 50 per cent displacement, to generate a net increase in output of £0.5 billion.

Finally, they regard a value of 1.3 as a more realistic multiplier, where a net increase of £0.5 billion would generate about 5,700 manufacturing jobs and increase employment by 7,500. However, O'Malley (1995) found that each manufacturing job in the South supports approximately one more job in the service sector, implying a multiplier well above 1.3 but below 2.

The most outstanding feature of the Scott and O'Reilly data is the dramatic difference between home sales per capita in each separate Irish region and the much lower sales per capita in the adjoining region. Scott and O'Reilly's analogy with Denmark and Sweden is perfectly relevant if we continue to regard North and South as being separate political and commercial jurisdictions with no likelihood of ever changing what has been until very recently a strained and remote relationship.[13] In the past, the Northern and Southern markets were segmented for many reasons, the most basic being an understandable fear, prior to the ceasefires, of travelling in the other jurisdiction to build up necessary commercial contacts.[14]

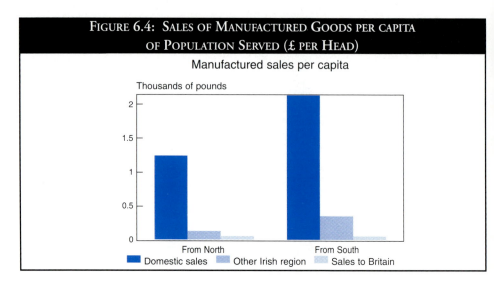

FIGURE 6.4: SALES OF MANUFACTURED GOODS PER CAPITA OF POPULATION SERVED (£ PER HEAD)

In the aftermath of peace the previous reluctance of individuals and groups to travel freely in both regions is rapidly coming to an end. Massively increased North-South tourist flows, and the pressure on the limited capacity of the Belfast-Dublin road and rail links, bear testimony to this process of rediscovery. However, there remain other reasons for continued market segmentation related to such issues as the different fiscal and monetary/exchange rate regimes, the separate and parallel functioning of public sector agencies like Forfás in the South and the IDB and LEDU in the North, with their obvious implications for higher business transaction costs when working in both markets.[15]

It is heartening to note that rapid progress is being made in addressing the problem of North-South market segmentation (D'Arcy and Dickson 1995). Southern literature is now targeted at disseminating information on Northern marketing opportunities (ABT 1994). An ambitious joint ABT/IDB initiative, supported by the International Fund for Ireland, has resulted in the publication of a detailed marketing guide to fifteen key product areas, facilitating greater North-South trade penetration as well as providing opportunities for import substitution. Joint promotions of Irish products overseas have been organized, and strategic alliances are being encouraged between Northern and Southern firms. The distribution system on the island, which has tended to deal with the North as part of the UK and with the South as a separate region, is gradually being integrated on an island basis (Molloy 1995). In the long term, the development of strategic transport links on an integrated all-island basis would be a powerful force for removing North-South market segmentation (Smyth 1995).

The potential gains from greater North-South trade interaction may be modest relative to the potential gains from greater penetration into wider world markets, including British markets. Nevertheless, there are gains to be made from intra-island trade in circumstances that will assist in strengthening the competitive performance of all businesses on this island. North-South trade improvement on this island is not an *alternative* to East-West trade improvement, but is entirely *complementary* to it. It is a transitional process that will produce gains in the short term and, by strengthening its supply-side, will help to position the island economy to make further advances in world markets.

The crucial economic issue in the future of North-South relations concerns whether developments like those described above should be left to the market or to piece-meal and ad hoc policy interventions. Some developments could be market led (e.g., trade promotion, etc.), but others (e.g., transport infrastructure) would seem to require a greater level of formal North-South coordination. Initial moves towards policy coordination on the island have been modest and more related to individual organizations (such as the island tourist boards and trade promotion agencies) than to any deeper policy redesign and harmonization. Nevertheless, the obvious enthusiasm of the private business sector for treating the island economy as a unit will bring its own pressures on the public policy-makers to move towards deeper cooperation and harmonization, thus opening the way for a transition to a more shared and coordinated form of faster island growth, to which we now turn.

6.3.2 Coordinated Development

The basic economic rationale behind any move towards a process of coordinated North-South development is implicit in our previous treatment of separate development. If it could be proved that the 'coordinated' option dominated the 'separate' option — in the sense of producing a better standard of living for all the people of the island — then there would at least be an economic logic for proceeding down the route of policy coordination, whatever about political consent to do so. Given the past histories of the two economies on the island and the limitations of ex ante economic analysis, there can be no such formal proof, but only an exploration of possibilities.

Two different attitudes to the future potential of policy coordination and business cooperation can be distinguished in the literature. On the one hand there are optimistic analyses that almost take it for granted that any move towards greater North-South cooperative linkages would produce large gains and opportunities for both parts of the island. A desire to provide a psychological boost to this process has led to proposals such as the development and strengthening of an economic corridor linking the two largest cities on the island, and the notion of a genuinely single island economy (Quigley 1992). Less optimistic analyses have been more concerned with the possibly limited gains to be had from reallocation of Northern security savings and are more sceptical about the role of peace in providing any sizeable boost to Northern growth (Gudgin 1995).

It has also been asserted that any government interference in a market-led process of North-South interaction, however modest, would generate inefficiencies. Perhaps if left to itself a free-market island economy would emerge and produce an optimal allocation of resources?[16] Certainly there are dangers that, even in cases of market failure, governments can do more harm than good.[17] But a combination of circumstances has ensured that free-market solutions have not been successful for North-South economics in the past and are unlikely to be any more successful in the future if a process of separate development continues.[18]

The separation of the island economy into two different political jurisdictions occurred with great acrimony in the early 1920s and led to minimal North-South economic interaction. This already low level of interaction was further damaged by the South's need to move to protectionism after 1932. The tentative moves towards closer contact during the 1960s (the O'Neill-Lemass era) were terminated by the outbreak of the troubles after 1968, events that generated understandable barriers to closer economic contact at a time when, ironically, both the North (as a region of the UK) and the South were about to become members of the EEC.

The political difficulties being experienced in getting all-party talks under way during the present peace process will also place obstacles in the way of any natural emergence of economic interaction since policy problems and other barriers still exist. Formal North-South policy coordination may now be needed, not in the old-fashioned Keynesian sense of simply increased public expenditure, but to promote market incentives and to remove barriers to normal economic interchanges that will be to the benefit of all the people of this island.

There is indeed a case for letting market forces operate and such forces are already operating strongly in a way that will begin to clarify the extent to which formal North-South policy coordination and institutions may be needed in the future. At one extreme, areas such as tourism may only need a modest level of formal inter-governmental cooperation on aspects such as joint marketing. In addition, key business organizations, such as IBEC in the South and the CBI in the North, can clearly begin a process of cooperation in the absence of formal North-South public policy harmonization. However, informal cooperation may very soon serve to identify areas where jurisdictional differences in policies and missing North-South institutions appear to be causing friction and may even be hindering or biasing growth on the island. An example of the former is the different corporate tax regimes for manufacturing, North and South, an aspect that the Chairman of the CBI(NI), Mr Doug Riley, drew attention to in his presentation to the Forum (Forum 1995, 24-25). An example of the latter is the need for policy cooperation and cross-border institutional arrangements if an initiative like the Belfast-Dublin Economic Corridor is to be implemented in a vigorous and effective manner that will accelerate growth on an islandwide basis.

What types of economic processes might benefit from North-South policy coordination? An obvious case is provided by the recent analysis of prospects for faster growth in Northern Ireland that was carried out by the group associated with the Northern Ireland Growth Challenge (NIGC 1995a and 1995b). This is a largely private sector initiative that is inspired by previous experience in the North in creating a dynamic industrial district in the north-east corner of the island during the second part of the nineteenth century. Motivated by the research findings of Michael Porter, the Growth Challenge wishes to promote policies that will replicate in the North the type of dynamic growth poles that have also motivated the analysis of the Culliton committee in the South and the North-South IBEC/CBI(NI) collaboration on the East Coast Economic Corridor initiatives. According to NIGC (1995a):

> There are clearly opportunities for Northern Ireland firms to become part of strong clusters, either developing locally or through networking with clusters which have been developing in GB or the Republic of Ireland. (P. 7.)

Specific examples of successful Southern clusters are identified by the Growth Challenge in sectors such as health technologies, computer software and hardware, and food processing. Identifying constraints on Northern competitiveness and growth, the Growth Challenge point to the South's low 10 per cent rate of corporate tax, wider British deindustrialization, the negative effects of the troubles on foreign direct investment, the insular/conservative culture and the 'protective' competiveness sapping role of traditional government policy.

In reading the Growth Challenge document one is struck forcibly by the parallels with the analysis of the Industrial Policy Review Group (the Culliton Report) in the South. Make a global 'search and replace' of 'Northern Ireland' by 'The Republic of Ireland' and little would have to be changed! If ever there was a good case for the Northern and Southern private and public sectors to coordinate their initiatives, this is it. Yet there is still only a limited formalized process through which ideas and proposals on economic policy can be exchanged. In the absence of such cooperation the process risks becoming a negative sum game of mutually damaging competition and missed opportunities rather that a positive sum game of cooperation.

An obvious reluctance of North and South to cooperate on industrial policy can be better understood in the light of the highly competitive nature of the process of attracting inward direct investment. To expect the IDA and IDB to cooperate closely is perhaps like expecting two football teams to cooperate in sharing out the spoils of the cup final. It is an unfortunate fact of life that in the business of attracting foreign industries to either of the two regions of this island, there are seen to be winners and losers. Indeed, even *within* each region, such attitudes are prevalent!

Once one turns, however, to the process of growing indigenous industry on the island, the role of North-South cooperation may replace beggar-thy-neighbour competition. Here there can be winners without losers. A wide range of policies and other issues interact in a way that could be mutually beneficial to both regions. Such areas include the capitalization and research costs of indigenous industry, where there may be scope for building on the presently weak scope of the Irish Stock Exchange and for encouraging the redirection of Irish pension funds towards the stimulation of indigenous firms. Other issues would relate to factor requirements, needs in respect of transfers of information by telecommunications and of intermediate products by enhanced island transport modes. There are obvious implications for policy harmonization in such areas as taxation policy and incentives, telecommunications and transport links and provision and coordination of education and training programmes. The cooperative development model of economic governance would appear to best meet these needs.

A New Framework for Agreement, drawn up by the British and Irish Governments, proposes that new institutions should be created 'to cater adequately for present and future political, social and economic inter-connections on the island of Ireland, enabling representatives of the main traditions, North and South, to enter agreed dynamic, new, co-operative and constructive relationships.' Besides the obvious rationale of such institutions in terms of common interest, mutual advantage and mutual benefit, the issue of economies of scale and avoidance of unnecessary duplication of effort is particularly noted. Cooperative development embraces such notions and differs from them only in the sense that North-South bodies should involve both public and private sector interests and should be specifically targeted at areas where present Northern and Southern policy structures are in economic conflict and where free-market solutions have not worked.

One of the beneficial consequences of North-South policy harmonization is that the growth processes in the North and South could become interrelated, even if both will remain crucially dependent on East-West linkages to larger world markets and external direct investment. Strengthening North-South linkages will be more important on the supply side than on the demand side. The total island of Ireland market will always be much smaller than the potentially huge international marketplace, so growth of conventional North-South cross-border trade will have a limited impact at best. The pay-off from deeper North-South supply-side linkages will come from the growth of Irish multinationals, who have drawn on the strengths of the coordinated island marketplace to grow domestically and progress to export markets in the classic growth process that Michael Porter portrays in his influential book, *The Competitive Advantage of Nations*. If the Belfast region was able to grow in this way in the late nineteenth century, one can have at least some degree of confidence that the coordinated island of Ireland economy could succeed in the late twentieth century. This could be ultimately the dividend that peace will deliver and upon which policy-makers should focus.

6.3.3 COORDINATION AND THE BELFAST-DUBLIN ECONOMIC CORRIDOR

Although the Coopers & Lybrand/Indecon feasibility study of the Belfast-Dublin Economic Corridor did not consider wider public policy issues of North-South co-ordination, the corridor proposal provides an excellent example of both the need for and potential benefits from such coordination. The main recommendations made in the feasibility study report fall under four broad headings:

- *Infrastructure*: a dramatic improvement in the quality of road and rail links between Belfast and Dublin, elements of which are already incorporated into the Northern and Southern Structural Fund programmes.

- *Development of business and other linkages*: through concessionary telecommunication tariffs, fiscal incentives to encourage North-South business collaboration, and improved dissemination of business information.

- *Specific development initiatives*: in selected business sectors and in the third level system.

- *Establishment of a task force to develop the corridor area.*

Although the feasibility study goes to great pains to stress that corridor development should not be pursued at the expense of other parts of the island, nevertheless we have seen earlier the tensions that previous policy initiatives favouring concentration can generate. However, if no such concentration is intended, then the corridor idea loses much of its power and becomes a modest local or regional initiative. Such tensions need to be addressed openly in public forums.

The feasibility study also stresses that its recommendations do not assume 'some massive structured plan involving large amounts of public expenditure'. Unfortunately, most of its recommendations have direct or indirect implications for public expenditure and North-South policy coordination. Most obvious is the large-scale infrastructure expenditure presently under way in the corridor area that is being financed under the Structural Funds for the period 1994-99 and is part of an island-wide improvement of infrastructure. Since these plans were decided outside the corridor framework, and essentially by reference to the pre-ceasefires situation, it would be interesting to see in what way the post 1999 level of corridor infrastructure will even begin to approach that of the more successful international corridors. This highlights the weak level of existing policy coordination in the general area of North-South infrastructure (Smyth 1995).

In the short term, North-South economic cooperation is likely to focus on more obvious areas such as tourism, export promotion, import substitution and savings from rationalization of energy utilities. Advances here are likely to be market driven, with the two Governments as facilitators rather than prime movers. The heavily populated corridor area is likely to be a major beneficiary. Indeed, success in these areas in the short to medium term could set the stage for long-term thinking about the island economy.

In the long term, North-South synergies are likely to arise from a more rational development of island infrastructure (where the South lags considerably behind the North), a widening and deepening of the education and training systems (where the South would appear to have an edge over the North), and a re-examination of the scope for regional policy in maximizing the returns from increased infrastructural and educational expenditures. Advances here are almost certainly going to be policy driven, and are likely to require the type of cross-border institutions envisaged in *Frameworks for the Future*. The coordination and planning needs of such wide-ranging initiatives simply could not be handled adequately by purely market driven private sector initiatives.

More specifically, any attempts to exploit the concept of clustering in developing the Belfast-Dublin corridor, or any other likely area, will require a mixture of private sector business and sectoral initiatives together with public planning and expenditure. Even within a single jurisdiction this would be complicated enough since it resurrects the debate on concentration versus dispersal previously examined by Buchanan (see chapter 5 above). But the corridor area spans two separate jurisdictions, with widely different fiscal, monetary and industrial policy frameworks. Hence, a whole new set of problems will arise that will take hard work, patience and good will to overcome.[19]

Within the corridor initiative there are two separate though interrelated strands:

1. Initiatives that will be the responsibility of the *private sector* alone and that can proceed immediately, against the background of existing public policy frameworks and expenditure plans, making best use of existing fiscal incentives. The CBI/IBEC corridor coordinating unit proposed in the feasibility study would seem ideal for this area of activity.

2. Initiatives that will require strong and concerted intervention by the Northern and Southern *public authorities*, where the benefits of concentration on the

corridor area must then be evaluated within an islandwide context and costed against other regional policy alternatives, and where the many policy differences that presently exist between the two jurisdictions are addressed directly in a search for policy synergies.

We showed in chapter 5 above that public policies involving focus, selectivity and concentration tend to be difficult to sustain in Ireland. Irish policy-makers seem to have a strong preference for regional and local equity over economic efficiency, and express this preference through a clientelist political system. However, the small physical size of the island, together with advances in communications technology, hold out possibilities of diluting the strictly spatial element involved in clustering (which has been so divisive in the past in both the North and the South), replacing it with a concept that could easily embrace the whole island. It is quite possible for 'sectoral clusters' to develop within an islandwide industrial policy that seeks 'spatial' equity, and the Growth Challenge has focused particularly on such sectoral clusters. The relatively small size of the island of Ireland means that the concept of sectoral clustering will tend to overlap with the more traditional concept of geographical clustering.[20] Hence, within the island there no longer need be as serious a trade-off between economic efficiency and spatial equity as that permeating the Buchanan Report of the 1960s.

As noted by the Growth Challenge, the emerging Southern electronics agglomeration is displaying signs of self-sustaining, education driven growth, albeit still of a very qualified and dependent type. The food processing sector, where indigenous Southern firms show up as significant external investors in the Northern market, holds out similar possibilities for agglomeration economies, where the spatial allocation is likely to be related to sources of supply from the agricultural sector. The Northern tradition of light and heavy engineering, although it suffered a serious decline during the troubles, may hold out the possibility of deepening the sub-supply mechanisms within the island, an enriching process that has so far largely eluded the South's multinational, high technology-based industrialization.

In developing the corridor proposals a more detailed examination of the experience abroad should prove of particular use in designing private sector initiatives for Ireland and in getting a better idea of the types of North-South policy coordination and institutional arrangements that may facilitate synergistic island growth. For example, the Emilia-Romagna area of Northern Italy is famous for its synergistic clusters of SMEs producing broadly traditional industrial products and its wide range of supportive trade organizations (Best 1990, 203-226). Complementing the role played by local government in Emilia-Romagna are many inter-firm productive associations, financial and marketing consortia and collective service centres.[21] Similar institutional arrangements will be needed on this island if the Belfast-Dublin corridor area is to ever find the identity and cohesiveness that has eluded it in the past.[22]

In attempting to apply the lessons of the Emilia-Romagna (or 'Third Italy') region to Ireland, one must take into account the fact that the tradition of local government in Ireland, North and South, is very different from that in Italy. Local government in Ireland has never had the powers or the resources to facilitate the type of public-private sector interactions that are at the heart of the success of Emilia-Romagna. In addition, the organizations representing employers and trades unionists have not yet evolved to a stage where it would be feasible to take on the executive functions that are commonly handled by such organizations in Italy, Germany and elsewhere. Hence, the major role in facilitating and progressing cross-border initiatives like the corridor must rest with the national governments, who must decide what regional and local arrangements and institutions are required. It will not be an easy task.

6.3.4 A SINGLE ISLAND ECONOMY

In his speech to the 1992 Annual Conference of the (then) Confederation of Irish Industry, Sir George Quigley stated that: 'I find no difficulty with the proposition that Ireland is — or should be — an island economy.'

A case can be made that one of the main legacies of the unhappy history between the two parts of Ireland, and between Ireland and Britain, has been an inferior level of economic performance since partition. Indeed, the island as a whole continues to underperform today. The usual explanations and excuses stress factors that appear to be internal to the two regions (e.g., a lack of entrepreneurial spirit, the small size of domestic markets, a tradition of outmigration, civil unrest, etc.). In truth, many of these factors are related to an economic divide of the island that predated political partition by over half a century.

We saw in chapter 2 that Ireland's misfortune was that when the late Industrial Revolution arrived in the middle of the last century, it was largely confined to the north-east corner of the island, centred on Belfast. Although economic historians still debate the complex causes of this phenomenon, the fact remains that the sundering of the then engineering/industrial North from the agricultural/food processing South destroyed almost all possibility of building intra-island synergies. To a large extent, this is still the island economy that presents us with problems and challenges.

A misunderstanding of the idea of an island economy is that, literally, it seems to advocate an inward-looking insularity. However, Sir George Quigley challenges us to widen our understanding of the role of small regions and small States in the increasingly integrated global economy, drawing on the ideas of the Japanese business strategist, Kenichi Ohmae (1995), who wrote:

> In Adam Smith's day, economic activity took place on a landscape largely defined — and circumscribed — by the political borders of nation states: Ireland with its wool, Portugal with its wines. Now, by contrast, economic activity is what defines the landscape on which all other institutions, including political institutions, must operate. (P. 129.)

On the global economic map, the lines that now matter are those defining 'natural economic zones', that represent no threat to the political borders of any nation. The defining issue is that each such zone possesses, in one or other combination, the key ingredients for successful participation in the global economy as defined by Robert Reich(see 6.2). Political leaders, however reluctantly, must adjust to the reality of such zones if they are to nurture faster economic growth. A permanent peace would create an unprecedented opportunity for progress in the development (or redevelopment) of the island as an economic zone in the way Ohmae and Reich describe. Far from insularity, this is effective and relevant global thinking.

Will the invisible hand of the market guide both economic regions of the island towards an optimal level of economic cooperation and integration, or is the very visible, and often clumsy, hand of government needed? Here, the unionist viewpoint seems to favour market forces over any degree of formality in cross-border institutions and planning. Indeed, their political logic obliges them to assert that the present rather anaemic level of North-South economic cooperation is already optimal.

The opposite economic viewpoint is that the present stand-off between North and South is an example of a failure in markets, to which businesses and consumers must accommodate. An obvious physical example is the inability or unwillingness to interface the road planning systems on both sides of the border. Another manifestation is the comparatively low level of telecommunication traffic between Dublin and Belfast, compared with the high level between, say, Dublin and Cork. However, the most damaging economic incompatibility between North and South probably relates to the two very different industrial promotion systems on the island. This serves to perpetuate further an already high degree of industrial mismatch and works against the creation of all-important synergies.

Evolution from a process of separate development towards cooperative and coordinated development is a reasonably natural one, as we have seen above. Elements of North-South economic coordination are already beginning to arise as a direct result of the peace process and under enthusiastic pressure from the business sectors of both regions. However, further evolution from coordination to what we have termed a single island economy will be much more difficult and, if it ever takes place, is likely to be spread over an extended period of time. Nevertheless, since there is considerable overlap between the coordination and single island economy categories, such an evolution could be smooth and natural, particularly if accompanied by parallel evolution towards greater federalism within the wider European Union. Ultimately, coordination could phase into total harmonization of policy-making, where lack of such coordination imposes barriers of any kind to faster island growth.

Any move from a 'coordinated' island economy to a 'single' island economy will require the harmonization of nearly all aspects of fiscal, monetary, industrial and labour market policies. The context for such a process of harmonization between North and South will depend on the type of political settlement that is arrived at in regard to the North. Furthermore, it will be conditioned by the nature and extent of European Monetary Union and further evolution towards a federal Europe. In chapter 4 we characterized three possible alternatives for a single island economy, ranging from politically minimalist to politically maximalist, together with an intermediate case. Detailed treatment of the intermediate and maximalist cases would take us deep into complex and sensitive political matters, far beyond our economic brief. Nevertheless, it may be useful to sketch out some of the characteristics of each case from an economic, or political-economic point of view, bearing in mind that political consent will be central to choices made in this area.

The politically minimalist case is one where the North continues to be a region of the UK, with little or no local policy autonomy. In such a situation, the context of North-South policy harmonization would shift to the issue of policy harmonization between the Republic of Ireland (the South) and Britain. Although there remains scope to handle issues arising between the South and Britain on a bilateral basis, a more logical and encompassing context would be provided by the European Union.

Where both Britain and the South are full participants in an evolving EMU, such a process of policy harmonization within these islands simply becomes a subset of a wider European process. However, the debate on EMU taking place both within Britain and between Britain and the rest of the EU, gives one an insight into how economics and politics become interconnected, and how full policy harmonization ceases to be economics and becomes political.

Moves towards economic policy harmonization on the island of Ireland could be seriously disrupted if Britain and the Republic of Ireland chose different approaches to Economic and Monetary Union. For example, suppose the Republic of Ireland chose to enter a comprehensive form of EMU that involved adopting a single European currency, a unified European monetary policy, and strict adherence to European fiscal policy norms and guidelines. If Britain chose to stay outside such a union, preserving the right to operate its own monetary policy and to deviate from Maastricht-type guidelines, then serious problems could be created for North-South attempts at policy coordination.[23]

The Southern experience during the early stages of its adherence to the narrow band of the EMS (1979-86) showed just how long it can take for expectations to adjust to fundamental changes in monetary policy regimes. Hence, any uncertainty that endures about differences between British and Irish attitudes to EMU are likely to delay moves towards North-South economic integration, were such to be on the agendas of the authorities in both regions. In such a situation of uncertainty, the North would most likely retain its focus on British rather than EU policy as the most likely option for minimizing internal economic disruption. Thus, the North-South policy harmonization agenda would continue to be dominated by Northern Ireland's East-West agenda.[24]

Further important issues for the island of Ireland arise in the context of the above debate on the nature of the relationship between Britain and the EU. A criticism of moves towards EMU has been made by many US economists, who point to the absence of strong fiscal transfer mechanisms within the EU that could be used to smooth the impact of shocks that might affect some regions more than others (Krugman 1992). For example, the State of Massachusetts suffered very badly in the late 1980s and early 1990s because of a sharp decline in the older type of mini-computers (such as those manufactured by Digital) and a wider recession in the defence electronics and avionics industry. These were areas of particular specialization in Massachusetts and were typical of the high level of regional specialization that characterizes a federal nation like the US. However, the fiscal transfer system acted automatically to protect living standards in Massachusetts and served to mitigate the worst aspects of the recession.

The Republic of Ireland would be potentially more exposed within the EU after EMU since it would not have access to the levels of intra-UK fiscal transfers that serve to buffer UK regions (such as Northern Ireland) from asymmetric shocks.[25] Indeed, the experience of the North during the British recession that occurred in the aftermath of the Lawson boom in the late 1980s illustrates this point well. The level of British subvention protected the North from the full rigours of the recession. If, in addition, Britain reserved the right, and had the freedom of action, to devalue against the core EMU currencies, there could be very serious problems for the economy of the Republic of Ireland.[26]

Difficulties with policy harmonization between these islands, and the subset of North-South problems within this island, are regional examples of wider issues within the EU as it attempts to move down the road to full EMU and afterwards to forms of close political federation. Indeed, it has been suggested that the future development of Ireland's island economy offers the EU a unique 'laboratory' in which to work out some basic requirements for the continued evolution of the Union, so there is scope for policy influence in both directions (D'Arcy 1995).

For example, the 'cohabitation' issue between the UK and Ireland is likely to be more acute than perhaps along any other internal border within the EU, if the South joins in Monetary Union and the UK stays out. With respect to the Common Agriculture Policy (CAP), informal cooperation already occurs at Council level.[27] Would there, however, be advantage in extending this to the creation of a single island CAP or could it be intensified even where policies continued to be formulated and administered by separate bodies, North and South? How far would this be inhibited by the reality, in such circumstances, that two separate governments would have to make the decisions involved with their often not insignificant financial consequences? The Belfast-Dublin rail link is a selected priority of both parts of the island, but many decisions have yet to be taken to ensure the infrastructural investment is complemented by far greater operational efficiency. It has been suggested that there should be a single company set up to run the upgraded cross-border rail service (Smyth 1995, 184).

At another extreme, the politically maximalist case of the single island economy is one where both North and South would come together in a confederal, federal or united Ireland. Although some of the simple budgetary arithmetic of such arrangements has been explored by the New Ireland Forum, the likely preconditions for the maximalist case have never been demonstrated in any realistic way (New Ireland Forum, 1984). History teaches us that close political and institutional ties between regions tend to come about in situations where there is a high degree of trust. However, North-South relations, and particularly intercommunity relations within the North, are classical examples of what Francis Fukuyama has described as 'low-trust' societies (Fukuyama 1995).

Fukuyama uses the concept of trust to mean 'the expectation that arises within a community of regular, honest, and cooperative behaviour, based on commonly shared norms, on the part of other members of that community.' Communities depend on mutual trust and will not arise spontaneously without it. People who do not trust one another will end up cooperating only under a system of formal rules and regulations, which have to be negotiated, agreed to, litigated, and enforced. Fukuyama concludes that 'widespread distrust in a society ... imposes a kind of tax on all forms of economic activity, a tax that high-trust societies do not have to pay.'

The logic of our economic analysis in this report points to the politically maximalist case as the one most likely to optimize the potential of the *island* economy as distinct from the potentials of the two regions as *separate* entities. Thus, for example, operation of a single industrial promotion system would facilitate sectoral integration and clustering, public expenditure difficulties in the way of operating a single CAP regime would no longer exist, infrastructure planning would proceed in a unified and coherent way, and the risk of disruption of trade and economic integration by exchange rate fluctuations would be eliminated. However, it is impossible to quantify the economic benefits of such an arrangement relative to the minimalist case with any convincing degree of certainty. Rather, the maximalist case is only likely to be relevant if the two traditions on the island are able to build a sufficiently high degree of trust. The earlier stages of economic and business interaction between the two regions of Ireland are likely to assist in building this trust, but economic benefits in the narrow sense are never likely to be the main factor in determining how far political integration in the island proceeds.

An intermediate arrangement between the minimalist and maximalist cases would be one where the North achieved a high degree of administrative and economic policy-making autonomy and, having done so, freely chose to exercise its new found autonomy by working towards maximizing the economic benefits of the island economy. A necessary condition for this scenario would be a more balanced Northern public finance position, i.e., one where the subvention was at most about 5 per cent of Northern GDP. Ideally, such regional financial balance would be achieved at a high level of income per head, a level not too different from that of the South.

If the North remained constitutionally part of the UK, then a further necessary condition for evolution of a single island economy would be a common Irish and British approach to EU policy initiatives such as EMU.

If the North, however, were to achieve a form of devolution from Britain that effectively amounted to independence, then the single island economy could come about even in the context of British deviation from EMU.

In the latest Democratic Dialogue publication, Robin Wilson, in a striking phrase, points out that 'getting more Northern Ireland is linked, rather than antithetical, to getting more *all*-Ireland' (Wilson 1996). Notions of islandwide economies of scale and of scope urgently need to be researched and developed in the light of history and in view of the potential presently opening up for evolution of a single island economy. It is too easy to dismiss this potential lightly, emphasizing the small size of the island and the even smaller size of its two component parts. It is also too easy to assert that if such opportunities existed, they would have been previously realized between Britain and Ireland rather than between the two parts of Ireland (Roche and Birnie 1995). Recent insights into economic growth have emphasized what is called 'path dependence', i.e., that if a region embarks on a process of growth, then that success tends to feed on itself and expectations can become self-fulfilling. The three-stage evolutionary process we have described in this chapter is one way of exploring the possibilities for guiding the island economy along a path of self-sustained growth whose benefits accrue to all and to remove barriers that history has placed on realizing the island's potential.

7 CONCLUSIONS

7.1 LEARNING FROM THE PAST

The presence of two different political traditions on this island is often used as a reason why there could never be a politically united Ireland. In the sphere of economics there is an analogue of this point of view which asserts that the growth of two separate economies on the island during the nineteenth century makes economic integration or even policy coordination of little relevance to the island's real development problems.

Our brief exploration of the manner in which the island economy fractured during the nineteenth century should give pause for thought to adherents of a nationalist view of economic history that blames poor Southern economic performance and the strong growth of the north-east region on British exploitation and an anti-Irish bias. The extraordinary success of the Belfast industrial district during the second half of the nineteenth century was the result of many different factors that happened to combine together to produce a localized Irish Industrial Revolution.

Equally, our account of the subsequent stagnation and decline of the Belfast economy, based as it was on linen, shipbuilding and engineering, should give pause for thought to adherents of a unionist view of economic history that looks exclusively to the example of the British economy for guidelines in running the economy of Northern Ireland. If the nineteenth century success of Belfast holds lessons for the South, the late twentieth century example of the South also holds lessons for the North. One of the more profitable aspects of increased flow of information and ideas across the North-South border might be the ability to learn from each other's experience.

The more recent experiences of North and South also contain much of mutual interest. The British-inspired move towards privatization and market testing of all aspects of the public sector has generated worldwide attention, and the Northern aspects of this process are of great interest to Southern policy-makers. In the South the rhetoric of free-market economics is more muted, but nevertheless it has had a profound impact on Southern policy-making after the experiences of the 1970s and early 1980s. In addition, the South's recent experience with modernization in the context of a social partnership should have interesting implications for the North (O'Donnell 1995). Other aspects identified by Quigley (1995) include:

- the tension between 'natural economic zones' and existing national boundaries, that lies at the heart of all discussions of North-South cooperation;

- the challenge faced by policy-makers to ensure that the island has the potential to be such a zone, with more effective performance arising from a North-South collaborative strategy;

- the important role to be played by the improved physical and social infrastructure, particularly in the North, but also in the South;

- the search for policies that will launch indigenous industry on a process of self-sustaining growth, very likely involving intense inter-firm cooperation.

History tells us that the island of Ireland has not functioned as a 'natural economic zone' since about the middle of the nineteenth century. The advent of partition and subsequent political tensions within the North and between North and South served to keep the two economies separate, a process that was further exacerbated by the imposition of tariff barriers to protect domestic Southern industry. The economic policies that prolonged the Southern dependence on the British economy (e.g., the sterling link, high labour mobility, etc.), did not bring the North and South together in the same way. However much history indicates the great obstacles that may be placed on the path to realizing such an all-island natural economic zone, it does not exclude it for the future.

A side effect of not functioning as a natural economic zone is that the island physical infrastructure is badly integrated, particularly in the immediate hinterlands of the cross-border areas. This was partly a result of the relative poverty of both regions, prior to the full policy integration of the North with Britain that occurred in the 1950s. But it also arose through the neglect of cross-border planning and, at least during the troubles, the disruption of cross-border access as a security response to paramilitary violence. The situation today is more optimistic, with major improvements in the island's infrastructure and with coordinated North-South movements under the auspices of the EU's Community Support Framework (Structural Funds) and INTERREG programmes.

Finally, history points to the very poor performance of indigenous industry on the island during the twentieth century and the role played by foreign direct investment. Although there are many different reasons for this behaviour, at least some of the blame can be attributed to the failure of the island economy to develop as a geographically integrated whole.

7.2 REALISTIC EXPECTATIONS FOR THE FUTURE

Five to ten years of peaceful growth could lead to a complete transformation of the Northern economy, in ways that we should not prejudge, and which are likely to have entirely beneficial spill over effects for the South. There will be peace dividends under all three of our evolutionary North-South economic policy strategies. Unfortunately, prior attitudes to all three, be they those of unionists or nationalists, are likely to be self-fulfilling. Thus, we must expect that the emergence of an optimal level of North-South economic policy coordination will be highly constrained by existing political, economic and cultural attitudes.

Although our study examines broad policy alternatives for the island, it cannot deal with these alternatives at the required level of institutional and policy detail. The rich research agenda we have identified must have one feature that is more important than all others, namely, it must be carried out in the full spirit of an island economy, or at least take the island dimension very seriously. This is not the case today, although much of the initial research could be viewed as a means of clearing away misconceptions and simply spreading knowledge of both regions throughout the island economy (D'Arcy and Dickson (eds) 1995; Bradley (ed.) 1995).

The island research agenda will need to examine a wide range of factors, such as:

- Exploration of the need for and the role of North-South institutions, where, however, the desirability of a North-South perspective must not be at the expense of East-West developments, particularly with Britain.

- The role to be played by EU policy; differences between the South and Britain; the EU as a catalyst to break an island log-jam, since it has the means and the powers.

- The wider global context of the island economy.

- Specific sector issues on a North-South axis, e.g., strategic alliances in public utilities, micro-level gains from trade, prospects for a dynamic North-South economic corridor, labour market and education cooperation, indigenous sector growth, infrastructural coordination.

Turning to possible benefits of peace, under all three alternatives, the peace dividend is likely to have four main elements that are interrelated in a way that will require later detailed quantitative analysis.

First, the inevitable restructuring of the balance between the public and private sectors in the North, not all of which is security-related, is likely to give a positive stimulus to the private sector through a more economically efficient allocation of public expenditure throughout the economy (KPMG 1995). Of course, the expected gains will only be produced if budgetary savings are recycled in large part.

Second, tourism in the North is displaying strong growth both as a result of peace and as the synergies between the two previously isolated parts of the island are being realized. The early stages of this recovery process will be of a transitional type, where the North will eventually reach a level of tourism earnings that mirrors the equivalent more 'normal' performance of Southern tourism. However important tourism is to the transition process, it is unlikely to play a major role in generating a permanent rise in the rate of economic growth.

Third, the recovery and growth of foreign direct investment in the North will be central to the promotion of a sustained increase in economic growth on the island. The process could be accelerated if Northern and Southern development agencies use this opportunity to promote a strengthening of the indigenous industrial and service sectors that has eluded both regions over the past thirty years. If such potential benefits of wider North-South cooperation can be realized in practice, growth rates in the two Irish regions could become consistently higher than in the case of separate development. In addition, growth in the island economy is likely to be higher in the medium to long term than in the more mature economies of Britain and the rest of the core EU members. This would hold out prospects for a reversal of almost a century of poor economic performance on the island and convergence of both regions to average EU standards of living.

Finally, the recent dramatic surge in North-South business contacts, and the deepening IBEC/CBI(NI) initiatives, hold out the prospects for development and strengthening of the indigenous industrial and service sectors that have proved difficult to achieve in the past. In a purely economic sense, Gorecki (1995b) suggests an interesting analogy that the troubles could be viewed as a non-tariff barrier to trade and investment between the two parts of Ireland. Having reviewed the international literature in the trade liberalization area, he suggests several factors that need to be examined in the context of the peace process: trade and investment; scale economies on the island; the role of external ownership of manufacturing industry; and the structure of industry.

Another aspect of the peace process concerns possible gains from greater inter-governmental cooperation and competition. In particular, Gorecki (1995b) suggests that there is a need to set policy rules that might overcome the very different incentive schemes used to attract foreign industry: mainly subsidy-based in the North and mainly tax-based in the South. For example, it is suggested that such rules might be modelled after some of the joint dispute resolution mechanisms that form part of the Canada-US Free Trade Agreement or the panels appointed to resolve differences under the General Agreement on Tariffs and Trade, where the existing EU mechanisms are not appropriate or adequate (Gorecki 1995b, 26).

KPMG (1995, 96-97), however make the point that any such supervisory operation would not be an easy task. They point out that in Britain, despite a strong central coordinating role played by the Department of Trade and Industry and oversight maintained by the Treasury, competition between regions for inward investments is intense. Indeed, there are frequent examples of one British region bidding against another and of liberal interpretations of the rules under which the organizations and agencies are supposed to operate. KPMG comment that any body which sought to oversee the inward investment activities of the IDA and IDB would need to have strong political backing and a highly effective information system. This view seems correct in regard to competition for individual investment projects. It may be, however, that the two agencies and the authorities, North and South, could aim at agreeing to lower the general value, as a percentage of investment, of the systems of incentives in both jurisdictions. How far this may be possible will depend on the assessment of the keenness of competition from incentives available in other locations, in Britain, continental Europe or elsewhere. But to the extent that co-operation on this basis was successful, it would bring about a reduction in future government expenditure on industrial promotion.

Even negative aspects of the island economy may come to be looked at with more optimism. It cannot have escaped attention that since the scale and characteristics of Northern and Southern unemployment have much in common, then perhaps the underlying causes and eventual solutions have much in common as well. In the North, the unemployment problem has an important regional dimension that coincides with the community divide (Murphy and Armstrong 1994). Policy in the South appears to have been more successful in addressing regional imbalances, particularly through the dispersal of foreign plants throughout the country. Northern policies appear to have been less successful in dealing with regional unemployment. Both regions suffer from local unemployment black spots, especially in urban areas, so future island policy will need to balance economic efficiency against the desirability of spatial equity.

We have already drawn attention to the fact that the preoccupation of this study with the North-South policy axis seems to fly in the face of the much stronger East-West links that both the Northern and Southern economies have with Britain and the rest of the world. From that wider world economy come most of the influences and forces that the small Irish economies have to adapt to and accommodate. But, as O'Donnell (1995) has pointed out, policy-making in a very internationalized economy requires focus on those areas where a very small country or region can still have some influence on its economic prosperity. Such areas of influence essentially come down to supply-side policies — education, training, technology, science, infrastructure, innovation and flexibility. Our study has argued that the North-South axis is an appropriate focus for all-island advances in these areas. Future research may perhaps show more conclusively that the island of Ireland is a natural economic zone and whether economies of scale, externalities etc., relate more to an all-island context than to, say, the wider British or EU contexts.

Under all three policy structures the peace dividend is likely to have many different and interrelated elements. However, two classes of peace dividends should be carefully distinguished: transitional adjustment effects and permanent growth effects. The most important example of the first kind of transitional adjustment effects will be associated with the inevitable restructuring of the balance between the public and private sectors in the North. This is likely to be at worst a zero-sum game, if budgetary savings are recycled, and probably a positive sum game (KPMG 1995).

A crucial issue for the future is whether the present modest North-South links can be developed to become an additional driving force for mutually reinforcing and beneficial growth in our island economy. Given the complexities, uncertainties and sensitivities involved, there can be only modest optimism at this stage. In reflecting on the economics of the island, we had in mind the admonitions of Charles Haughey to economists in general, and to Sir Charles Carter and Professor Louden Ryan in particular, after their presentations to the New Ireland Forum on 21 September 1983. Mr Haughey complained that economists 'could not formulate for us in this Forum a prospect of an all-Ireland economic entity capable of developing its own inherent dynamic for progress provided the political structures are right.' In these more peaceful and hopeful times the exploration can be more imaginative and free-ranging, the questions can be franker, and the answers need not be so pessimistic.

At a time of peace in this island, when hope burns bright after twenty five years of violence, we are reminded of the uncharacteristically sombre words of the great economist, John Maynard Keynes, who had watched with mounting disquiet the leaders of the great powers attempt to broker a lasting peace at Versailles in 1919. At the conclusion of *The Economic Consequences of the Peace* he wrote:

> The events of the coming year will not be shaped by the deliberate acts of statesmen, but by the hidden currents, flowing continually beneath the surface of political history, of which no one can predict the outcome. In one way only can we influence these hidden currents — by setting in motion those forces of instruction and imagination which change *opinion*. The assertion of truth, the unveiling of illusion, the dissipation of hate, the enlargement and instruction of men's hearts and minds, must be the means.

These feelings have been echoed by the former President of the Commission of the European Communities, Jacques Delors, in his preface to *The European Challenges Post-1992*:

> What is also cruelly lacking today is the ability to generate new visions. Because there is no vision, tension and wariness are rife, putting a real brake on economic activity. In the 1990s, we have more to fear from deficient levels of cooperation, political will and imagination than from any other form of scarcity.

APPENDIX
NORTH-SOUTH ECONOMIC RESEARCH

1.1 KEY THEMES IN NORTHERN AND SOUTHERN ECONOMIC RESEARCH

Since policy-makers in the South have a wider range of instruments to play with, and given the more extensive range of available Southern data, it is not surprising that Southern economic and econometric research reflects a greater diversity than in the North. During the 1970s a major theme of Southern research concerned international price transmission and a series of pioneering papers established firmly the external source of most Southern price inflationary pressures (Geary 1976). However, after the link with sterling was broken, price determination issues became more complex. Work by Callan and FitzGerald (1989) re-established the external price-taking findings for the exposed traded sector, although, with the recent turbulence of the EMS the issues are still controversial.

The Southern inflation transmission literature finds no parallel in Northern Ireland. Indeed, Northern price data are almost impossible to come by since the statistical fiction is widely maintained that Northern prices are identical to those of the UK. Hence, Northern external price determination must go far beyond the traded sector and apply to the non-traded sector as well as to an extensive area of wage determination (Roper and Schofield 1990).

During the 1980s there was considerable econometric work on the supply-side of the Southern economy, much of it based on formal production and cost functions (Bradley, FitzGerald and Kearney 1993). It was established that the notion of internationally mobile investment was at the centre of the behaviour of the Southern manufacturing sector and the ability to attract this investment depended on Southern costs of production (in particular wage costs) and the profitability of firms in the South relative to other international locations (Bradley and FitzGerald 1988). Even for indigenous firms, the ability to survive depended on a similar competitiveness calculus.

Not surprisingly, this theme finds echoes in Northern Ireland research (Borooah and Lee 1991; Roper and Schofield 1990). Indeed, with the deepening of EU economic integration, the larger member States will increasingly begin to display regional characteristics similar to the Republic of Ireland and Northern Ireland.

Given the serious unemployment problems in both regions, one would expect to find in Ireland as rich a macroeconomic and microeconomic empirical literature on the labour market as, say, that of Britain, summarized and integrated in Layard, Nickell and Jackman (1991). While there have been some recent econometric studies of unemployment, they raise many more questions than they answer and the area is still under-researched (see Geary 1988 for a general survey of the field; Kennedy 1993 is a recent non-technical examination of the main issues in the South; Gorecki 1995a provides an analysis of the Northern situation).

In two recent studies, Newell and Symons (1990) and Barry and Bradley (1991) used econometric modelling techniques to try to answer the following question: Why did the Republic of Ireland's rate of unemployment rise by 10 percentage points between 1979 and 1987 and lock into the higher rate? The potential culprits were the slow-down in the world economy (particularly the deterioration in the British labour market in the first half of the 1980s), domestic policy actions and demographic trends. Barry and Bradley attributed the blame equally to the world recession of 1979-81 and its aftermath, and the high tax rates needed to stabilize the burgeoning Southern national debt after the fiscal expansions of the earlier 1977-82 period.[1]

Of interest in the Barry and Bradley study is the so-called 'hysteresis' effect of rising unemployment on wage bargaining. It was found that while the unemployment rate is rising, it exerts downward pressure on wage inflation, but when unemployment stabilized, even at a high level, the numbers of long-term unemployed build up and tend not to continue to participate effectively in the labour market. Hence, upward pressure on wage inflation can coexist with high levels of aggregate unemployment where a sizeable fraction of it is long term. Also, increases in labour productivity were found to be mainly passed on to labour in the form of higher wages, a result replicated in most other EU countries but not at all the case in the US labour market (Dreze and Bean 1990). In summary, this research has serious implications for the prospects of ever reducing the rate of Southern unemployment even to the already high average EU levels in the absence of major changes in the mechanisms of wage bargaining and in the nature of the system of unemployment transfer payments and retraining.

In a related study, Borooah and Lee (1991) examined disparities of economic performance between Northern Ireland and Britain. They proceeded from the hypothesis that such regional disparities arise as the consequence of regional differences in cost competitiveness. In summary, they found that lower total factor productivity (TFP) growth in the North compared with Britain coincided with a rapid convergence of Northern wage rates upwards towards those in Britain. This had serious negative consequences for Northern manufacturing competitiveness, employment and unemployment. They also found that the level of the capital stock had little influence on employment and Northern demand for labour was considerably more sensitive to the real wage level than is the case in Britain. Factors affecting the demand for labour had little effect in wage determination: rather, Northern wages are determined by British wages, moderated to a modest degree by local labour market conditions.

These two islands have long constituted a single market for labour, even in times of economic disruption such as during the tariff wars of the 1930s. This heavily influences the way in which one models the two Irish regional labour markets, and emphasizes the role of labour migration to an extent that is unique in OECD modelling literature. Labour mobility implies that the Northern and Southern rates of unemployment tend to move in tandem with British rates, other things being equal. Hence, tension (or Phillips curve) effects in the two Irish wage bargaining models are rapidly attenuated if the Irish regions are subjected to external or domestic disturbances. Otherwise, wage determination differs between the two regions, with essentially a one-for-one relationship between Northern and British wage inflation but a more complex bargaining process in the South, driven by producer prices, a tax wedge and sectoral productivity (Barry and Bradley 1991).

More generally, given the largely external determination of all tradable prices in the island of Ireland, the only flexibility left relates to the price of labour (for North and

South) and the exchange rate (for the South only), where the latter has seldom been availed of in practice. Further investigation will be needed to establish how the two regions of Ireland fit into the pattern of British regional labour market behaviour (Blackaby and Manning 1990). However, what experience with Irish regional modelling points to is that the behaviour of inter-regional labour mobility has much wider implications than just for the regional labour market, but affects the whole behaviour of the regional macroeconomy.

In summary, then, there is much to be learned from the econometric research findings for North and South. We have merely touched on this work, stressing the mechanisms of price transmission, wage determination, unemployment, competitiveness and the operation of the supply-side of the economy. In addition, there are interesting results concerning the determinants of household consumption, investment in residential property, and, at least in the case of the South, work on the operation of the financial and money markets. There remains much scope for systematizing this work and for carrying out a more in depth North-South comparison.

1.2 NORTHERN AND SOUTHERN ECONOMIC MODELLING

The goal of much applied econometric research is the construction of complete computer-based model systems to describe an economy, and there are two existing operational large-scale macro-models of the Irish regional economies: NIMOD in the North (Roper and Schofield 1990) and HERMES in the South (Bradley and FitzGerald 1991). Both models are highly disaggregated, having considerable sectoral and expenditure detail (twenty five production sectors in NIMOD and eleven in HERMES). They were constructed in isolation from each other, have distinct specific features and, consequently, are of limited value for comparative work on the two economies.[2]

The broad underpinnings of NIMOD come quite naturally from the position of the North as a region within the UK. This explains NIMOD's neglect of balance of trade and public sector financing constraints (quite aside from data difficulties, which can usually be overcome in one way or another). Also, investment behaviour is passive in NIMOD and not modelled behaviourally. The focus on Britain as the entire external 'world' environment for the North and the largely external wage/price mechanisms are partially the result of a purely regional perspective, but research is made more difficult by missing data.

For the Southern HERMES model, the underpinnings come from the South's status as an independent sovereign State with a small open economy. This necessitates careful attention to trade, balance of payments and public sector financing constraints. The greater diversification (compared with the North) of trade away from Britain and towards EU and other world markets, together with the non-British source of most foreign direct investment, requires a wider international orientation of the model than is the case in NIMOD, and the available Southern data permit such an approach. Finally, since the break in the Irish pound link with sterling in 1979, there has been considerable scope for wider domestic and international price/wage influences in the South. Although tradable prices essentially remain externally determined (in the context of the South's quasi-fixed EMS-based exchange rate regime), non-traded prices are determined internally as a mark-up on costs, and there are considerable domestic influences on wage bargaining mechanisms.

Both NIMOD and HERMES have some shared core stylized features. For example, both are in the neo-Keynesian tradition in that disequilibria (like unemployment) can arise and persist and wages and prices do not move rapidly to clear markets. They both use backward-looking or auto-regressive expectations mechanisms, and they are aggressively open in orientation in both product and labour markets. Finally, they are similar in broad sectoral structure, each model consisting of the following categories:

- A range of exposed manufacturing sectors, which are price taking and driven mainly by external demand.

- A range of sheltered service sectors, which (only in the South) determine their prices as a mark-up on costs and are driven by internal regional demand.

- An agriculture sector that is dominated by the EU Common Agriculture Policy (CAP).

- Broadly similar public sector categories and organization, but considerable differences in the levels of tax rates, social expenditure and funding mechanisms.

HERMIN and NIMIN: Two New Regional Models of Ireland

The situation with respect to the existing NIMOD and HERMES models is that they are very large and complex, have very specific features, and are silent on some important issues. The missing features mainly relate to the Northern model, NIMOD. Although both models are very useful for work on the two regions separately, they are not suitable for work on comparing and contrasting the two regions.

For the reasons outlined above, and building on previous research, new, small scale, neo-Keynesian macro-models of the two regional economies of Ireland have been constructed at the ESRI: NIMIN for the North and HERMIN for the South. These are experimental aggregate core models, have a common level of sectoral disaggregation, and similar theoretical assumptions. For detailed technical descriptions of these models the reader is referred to the relevant literature (Bradley, Whelan and Wright 1993 for HERMIN and Bradley and Wright 1992 for NIMIN).

The production sides of HERMIN and NIMIN are disaggregated into four sectors, this division being the very least needed to obtain a clear picture of the structure and dynamics of open regional economies like Ireland, North and South:

1. An aggregate internationally traded sector (T), excluding agriculture, consisting of all manufacturing industry.

2. An aggregate private/market non-traded sector (N), consisting of market services, building and construction and utilities.

3. Agriculture, forestry and fishing (A).

4. A non-market/public, service sector (G).

For material on the use of the HERMIN and NIMIN models, see Bradley, Whelan and Wright 1993; Bradley and Wright 1992.

1.3 POLICY ANALYSIS USING NORTHERN AND SOUTHERN MODELS

The main motivation in constructing HERMIN and NIMIN is to work towards a better understanding of the structures and growth processes of the two Irish regional economies, and to be in a better position to analyse the medium- to long-run effects of exogenous policy and world shocks. To illustrate the use of the Irish models, we examine three types of shock: a boost to public consumption, an increase in world growth activity and an increase in the British rate of unemployment, the latter being of special relevance to the performance of the two Irish labour markets. Specifically, we examine shocks to the following variables that are exogenous to HERMIN and NIMIN:

- A public expenditure shock consisting of a permanent increase in public sector employment of 10,000 above the baseline in both models.

- A 1 per cent permanent increase in world output above the baseline.

- A 1 percentage point increase in the UK unemployment rate above the baseline.

These three shocks illustrate certain symmetries and asymmetries of the economies of the North and South. First, attempts to stimulate regional activity through increased regional public consumption can have enduring benefits in the case of the North, where any tax financing is carried by the entire UK. In the South, such a shock would have similar effects if the source of finance was in the form of, say, an EU-funded transfer. In each case the fiscal multiplier is small, and never rises above 1.3.

However, if the Southern public authorities attempted to carry out such a demand stimulus, it will have a much more attenuated impact, since any required tax financing must be carried by the small Southern tax base. Any such rise in tax rates will depress domestic demand, increase the tax wedge, drive up wage inflation and cause a loss of international competitiveness. The resulting multiplier falls from an impact value of about 1.3 to near zero as the public sector crowds out the private sector. If the Northern increase in public employment were to be financed within a fixed subvention, the regional analogue of a balanced budget, a similar attenuation of the multiplier would occur.

Second, the benefits of increased 'world' demand are stronger in the South, with its larger manufacturing sector (34 per cent of GDP) and consequentially stronger indirect demand responses, than in the North, where the manufacturing sector has shrunk to half its size over the last twenty years and now generates only about 20 per cent of GDP. Consequently, a 1 per cent sustained increase in world demand generates a 0.5 per cent increase in Southern GDP, but a less than 0.3 per cent GDP increase in the North.

Third, the different speeds of adjustment of the two regional labour markets in response to higher unemployment in the British labour market are quite marked and arise from the dynamics in the migration equation. The econometric evidence suggests that the speed of adjustment in the South is about three times that of the North, although more precise investigations will be needed to establish this firmly.

The above analysis is very partial in nature and can, as a consequence, be misleading. For example, it is very unlikely that the British rate of unemployment would ever rise in the absence of other associated changes in the British economy, such as lower output, wages and prices. Hence, we need to examine some slightly more realistic external shocks that take into account possible linkages between the external variables. The key external 'driving' variables in HERMIN and NIMIN consist of output, prices, unit labour costs and interest rates in the wider world economy; the British unemployment rate and the British wage rate. The world variables operate mainly through the exposed traded sector while the British unemployment rate operates directly through the two Irish regional labour markets. The externally determined interest rates have a wide range of channels of influence, through the cost of capital to firms, housing investment, national debt interest, etc.

Two of the shocks considered above, those of world output and the British rate of unemployment, were partial in nature because they considered the multiplier effects of changing just one external variable in NIMIN/HERMIN, holding all the others constant, thus ignoring how such shocks might actually arise in the world economy and possible associations between external variables which are interrelated in the context of the wider world economy. A better analysis needs to use a two-stage process. At the first stage, one can use a model of the 'world' economy to simulate the effects of exogenous shocks at the world level on all the variables that are external in the two Irish models. At the second stage one can simulate HERMIN and NIMIN using the changed configuration of external variables generated at the first stage within a world model, such as the NIESR's NIGEM.

Such a two-stage process is valid because the peripheral satellite HERMIN and NIMIN models are post-recursive to the larger NIGEM model. Hence, world events (analysed in the first stage of the world model simulations) influence the economies of the island of Ireland, but Irish events (analysed in the second stage NIMIN/HERMIN simulations) have little or no feedback influence on the rest of the world. This represents a simple strategy for linking the two Irish regional models into a larger encompassing world model while, at the same time, taking into account the interrelationships between the larger OECD big seven economies. However, at present there is a very serious limitation in model-based analysis of the island of Ireland, in that direct economic links between the North and South are not yet treated.

1.4 THE NEED FOR A NORTH-SOUTH ECONOMIC MODELLING FRAMEWORK

The HERMIN and NIMIN models allow one to explore fundamental theoretical choices in the following sense. The eventual goal is to link the two regional *Irish* models to a world model (for example, the London-based National Institute of Economic and Social Research (NIESR) global economic model, NIGEM) and to each other. This will be greatly facilitated by having compatible parallel models for the two Irish regional economies like HERMIN and NIMIN. Linking the new models to each other in the context of the world economy will permit important issues to be explored:

- Can import leakages out of the island be lowered and the benefits of more intensive trade be realized along the lines of the CII claims discussed in chapter 6?

- How could a greater domestic 'island' market promote growth, moving beyond trading at arms length and building more supply-side linkages between the two regions (Porter 1990)?

- How can faster growth be financed, either through internal sources (Co-operation North 1991) or through external sources (e.g., the EU Structural Funds)?

- How would Irish industrial policy work if it were formulated and executed on an all-island basis?

- Specifically, what are the possible synergies from focusing economic development on the important Belfast-Dublin economic corridor, as initially suggested by Quigley (1992)?

- What would be the likely effects of externalities from infrastructure and training policies (Bradley, Whelan and Wright 1993)?

In addition, we need to be able to explore the consequences of regional trade and public finance imbalances. The need for such analysis in the South goes without saying. The justification is less obvious for the North, but nonetheless important. The North's relative policy autonomy within the UK needs to be analysed in the context of an imputed regional budget constraint. There are shadow costs within the

UK of increasing the North's 'block grant' which must be set off against any benefits. Even if these are not made explicit, they must surely be implicit in the Northern administration's negotiations with London.

Furthermore, if public policy in Northern Ireland is directed at increasing export oriented growth, then the net trade balance must be of interest since it represents the only true measure of the regional competitiveness outcome. Future extensions of NIMIN and HERMIN will need to look at wider concepts of regional competitiveness than are presently used.

Finally, a very serious gap in existing Irish regional models concerns the absence of any North-South interactions within the wider economy of the island of Ireland. In chapter 3 we pointed to the extensive North-South trade and the Southern trade surplus with the North. There is also a certain amount of North-South migration of labour, and some Southern ownership of Northern industry (NIEC 1992). Future developments will need, at the very least, to model the determinants of North-South trade and migration. Capital flows may be more difficult to model, as will be the benefits of a greater domestic island market in the promotion of faster growth, moving beyond trading at arms length and building more supply-side linkages between the two regions.

BIBLIOGRAPHY

Adams, Gerry 1995. *Free Ireland: Towards a Lasting Peace*, Dingle: Brandon Book Publishers.

Anderson, R., K. Frohlberg, M. Keyzer, et al. 1994. 'EC Agricultural Policy for the Twenty First Century'. *European Economy*, No. 4.

Armstrong, Harvey and Jim Taylor 1993. *Regional Economics and Policy* (2nd ed.), London: Harvester Wheatsheaf.

Bacon, Robert and Walter Eltis 1976. *Britain's Economic Problem: Too Few Producers*, London: Macmillan.

Baldwin, John R. and Paul K. Gorecki 1990. *Structural Change and the Adjustment Process: Perspectives on Firm Growth and Worker Turnover*, Ottawa: Supply and Services Canada.

Bardon, Jonathan 1982. *Belfast: An Illustrated History*, Belfast: The Blackstaff Press (reprinted with corrections, 1995).

— 1992. *A History of Ulster*, Belfast: The Blackstaff Press

Barry, Frank and John Bradley 1991. 'On the Causes of Ireland's Unemployment'. *Economic & Social Review* 22, No. 4, 253-286.

Best, Michael 1990. *The New Competition: Institutions of Industrial Restructuring*, Cambridge (UK): The Polity Press.

Blackaby, D. and D. Manning 1990. 'Earnings, Unemployment and the Regional Employment Structure in Britain'. *Regional Studies*. 24, 529-535.

Blake, Neil 1995. 'The Regional Implications of Macroeconomic Policy'. *Oxford Review of Economic Policy*. 11, No. 2, 145-164.

Bord Trachtála, An 1994. *Northern Ireland: A Market Profile*, Dublin: An Bórd Tráchtála.

Borooah, V.K. and K.C. Lee 1991. 'The Regional Dimension of Competitiveness in Manufacturing: Productivity, Employment and Wages in Northern Ireland and the United Kingdom'. *Regional Studies*. 25(3), 219-229.

Boyle, G.E. 1992. 'National Responses to the CAP Reform Proposals'. In *The Impact of Reform of the Common Agricultural Policy*. Report No. 92, Dublin: The National Economic and Social Council.

Bradley, James F., Victor N. Hewitt and Clifford W. Jefferson 1986. *Industrial Location Policy and Equality of Opportunity in Assisted Employment in Northern Ireland 1949-1981*. Research Paper 10, Belfast: Fair Employment Agency.

Bradley, James F. 1990. 'The Irish Economies: Some Comparisons and Contrasts'. In *The Northern Ireland Economy*. Eds, R. Harris et al., London: Longman.

Bradley, John and Connell Fanning 1981. 'Twenty Five Years of Macromodelling the Irish Economy: Retrospect and Prospect'. *Journal of the Statistical and Social Inquiry Society of Ireland* 24, 107-131.

Bradley, John, Connell Fanning, Canice Prendergast and Mark Wynne 1985. *Medium-Term Analysis of Fiscal Policy in Ireland: A Macroeconometric Study of the Period 1967-1980*. General Research Paper No. 122, Dublin: The Economic and Social Research Institute.

Bradley, John and John FitzGerald 1988. 'Industrial Output and Factor Input Determination in an Econometric Model of a Small Open Economy'. *European Economic Review* 32, 1227-1241.

— 1991. 'The ESRI Medium-Term Economic Model'. In *Medium-Term Review: 1991-1996*. Dublin: The Economic and Social Research Institute

Bradley, John, John FitzGerald and Daniel McCoy 1991. *Medium-Term Review: 1991-1996*. Dublin: The Economic and Social Research Institute, June.

Bradley, John and Karl Whelan 1992. 'Irish Experience of Monetary Linkages with the United Kingdom and Developments Since Joining the EMS'. In *Economic Convergence and Monetary Union in Europe*. Ed. R. Barrell, London: SAGE Publications in association with the NIESR.

Bradley, John and Jonathan Wright 1992. *NIMIN: A Small-Scale Structural Model of the Northern Ireland Economy*. Discussion Paper No IFI/NS 01/92, Dublin: The Economic and Social Research Institute.

Bradley, John, John FitzGerald and Ide Kearney 1993. 'Modelling Supply in an Open Economy using a Restricted Cost Function'. *Economic Modelling*. 10 January, No. 1, 11-21.

Bradley, John, Karl Whelan and Jonathan Wright 1993. *Stabilization and Growth in the EC Periphery: A Study of the Irish Economy*. Aldershot:Avebury.

Bradley, John and Karl Whelan 1995. 'The Irish Expansionary Fiscal Contraction: A Tale From One Small European Economy'. To appear, *Economic Modelling*.

Bradley, John, Nuala O' Donnell, Niamh Sheridan and Karl Whelan 1995. *Regional Aid and Convergence: Evaluating the Impact of Structural Funds on the European Periphery.* Aldershot: Avebury.

Bradley, John, Nuala O'Donnell and Niamh Sheridan 1995. 'Infrastructure, Human Resources and Competitive Advantage: Ireland, North and South'. in *The Two Economies of Ireland.* J. Bradley (ed.), Dublin: Oak Tree Press.

Breen, Richard, Damian Hannan, David Rottman and Christopher Whelan 1990. *Understanding Contempory Ireland.* Dublin: Gill and Macmillan.

Breen, Richard 1991. *Education, Employment and Training in the Youth Labour Market.* General Research Series, Paper No. 152, Dublin: The Economic and Social Research Institute.

Breen, Richard and Christopher Whelan 1995. 'Investment in Education: Educational Qualifications and Class of Entry in the Republic of Ireland'. Paper presented at the International Project on the Relationship Between Education and Social Class Mobility, European University, Florence, 23-26 March.

Brennan, Peter 1995. 'The European Union: The Island's Common Cause'. In *Border Crossings, Developing Ireland's Island Economy.* M. D'Arcy and T. Dickson (eds), Dublin: Gill and Macmillan.

Brunt, Barry 1988. *Western Europe Economic & Social Studies: The Republic of Ireland.* London: Paul Chapman Publishing.

— 'The New Industrialization of Ireland'. In *Ireland: Contemporary Perspectives on a Land and its People.* R. Carter and A. Parker (eds.), London: Routledge.

Cadogan Group 1992. *Northern Limits: Boundaries of the Attainable in Northern Ireland Politics.* Belfast: The Cadogan Group.

— 1994. *Blurred Vision: Joint Authority and the Northern Ireland Problem.* Belfast: The Cadogan Group.

— 1995. *Lost Accord: The 1995 Frameworks and the Search for a Settlement in Northern Ireland.* Belfast: The Cadogan Group.

Callan, Tim and John FitzGerald 1989. 'Price Determination in Ireland: Effects of Changes in Exchange Rates and Exchange Rate Regimes'. *Economic & Social Review* 20, 165-188.

Callan, T., B. Nolan, B.J. Whelan, D.F. Hannan and S. Creighton 1989. *Poverty, Income and Welfare in Ireland.* General Research Series, Paper No. 146, Dublin: The Economic and Social Research Institute.

Canning, D., B. Moore and J. Rhodes 1987. 'Economic Growth in Northern Ireland: Problems and Prospects'. In P. Teague (ed.), *Beyond the Rhetoric.* London: Lawrence and Wishart.

Cantillon, Sara, John Curtis and John FitzGerald 1994. *Medium-Term Review: 1994-2000*. Dublin: The Economic and Social Research Institute, April.

Castells, M. and P. Hall 1994. *Technopoles of the World: The Making of 21st Century Industrial Complexes*. London: Routledge.

Central Planning Bureau 1992. *Scanning the Future: A long-term scenario study of the world economy 1990-2015*. The Hague: Sdu Publishers.

Commission of the European Communities 1993. 'The economic and financial situation in Italy, Annex III: Regional disparities: the Southern issue'. *European Economy, Reports and Studies*, No. 1.

Compton, Paul 1995. *Demographic Review Northern Ireland 1995*. Research Monograph 1, Northern Ireland Economic Council, Belfast: Northern Ireland Economic Development Office, March.

Confederation of Irish Industry 1990. *Newsletter*, May.

Co-operation North 1991. *Potential Synergies in the Development of Financial Services North and South*. Third Study Series, Report No. 2, Belfast/Dublin: Co-operation North.

Coopers & Lybrand and Indecon 1994. *A Corridor of Opportunity: Study of Feasibility of Developing a Dublin-Belfast Economic Corridor*. Report prepared for IBEC/CBI(NI), Belfast and Dublin.

Crotty, Raymond 1986. *Ireland in Crisis: A Study in Capitalist Colonial Underdevelopment*. Dingle: Brandon Book Publishers.

D'Arcy, Michael and Tim Dickson (eds) 1995. *Border Crossings: Developing Ireland's Island Economy*. Dublin: Gill and Macmillan.

D'Arcy, Michael 1995. 'Ireland's island economy and the EU: a laboratory for future European evolution?' Address to a joint meeting of the Institute for European Affairs and the Northern Ireland Centre in Europe, Brussels, 2 October.

Deane, Seamus 1984. 'Remembering the Irish Future'. In *Ireland: Dependence and Independence*, Dublin: *The Crane Bag*, 81-92.

Department of Economic Development 1990. *Competing in the 1990s*. Belfast: Department of Economic Development.

— 1995. *Growing Competitively: A Review of Economic Development Policy in Northern Ireland*. Belfast: Department of Economic Development.

DKM Economic Consultants 1994. *The Economic Impact of the Northern Ireland Conflict*. Dublin: DKM Economic Consultants, January.

Dowling, Brendan 1974. 'Some Economic Implications of a Federal Ireland'. In *Economic and Social Implications of the Political Alternatives that may be Open to Northern Ireland*. N.J. Gibson (ed.), Coleraine: University of Ulster.

Dreze, J.H. and C.R. Bean 1990. 'Europe's Unemployment Problem: Introduction and Synthesis'. In *Europe's Unemployment Problem*, eds. J.H. Dreze and C.R. Bean, Cambridge: The MIT Press, 1-65.

Fanning, R. 1978. *The Irish Department of Finance 1922-58*. Dublin: The Institute of Public Administration.

Farley, Noel 1995. 'A Comparative Analysis of the Performance of the Manufacturing Sectors, North and South: 1960-1991'. In *The Two Economies of Ireland: Public Policy, Growth and Employment*, J. Bradley (ed.), Dublin: Oak Tree Press.

FitzGerald, J. 1986. *The National Debt and Economic Policy in the Medium Term*. Policy Research Series No. 7, The Economic and Social Research Institute, Dublin.

—1995. 'Babies, Budgets and the Bathwater'. *Irish Banking Review*, Summer, 18-32.

Folmer, C., M. Keyzer, M. Merbis, H. Stolwijk and P. Veenendaal 1995. *The Common Agricultural Policy Beyond the McSharry Reform*. Amsterdam: North-Holland.

Forum for Peace and Reconciliation 1995. *Report of Proceedings*, Vol. 3, Friday, 16 December 1994. Dublin: The Stationery Office.

Fukuyama, F. 1995. *Trust: The Social Virtues and the Creation of Prosperity*. Hamish Hamilton: London.

Geary, P.T. 1976. 'Lags in the Transmission of Inflation: Some Preliminary Estimates'. *The Economic and Social Review* 7, 383-389.

— 1988. *The Nature and Functioning of Labour Markets*. Paper No. 86, Dublin: The National Economic and Social Council.

Giavazzi, F. and M. Pagano 1991. 'Can Severe Fiscal Contractions be Expansionary? Tales of Two Small European Countries'. In *The NBER Macroeconomics Annual 1991*. Cambridge (Massachusetts): The MIT Press.

Gibson, Norman J. and John E. Spencer (eds) 1975. *Economic Activity in Ireland: A Study of Two Open Economies*. Dublin: Gill and Macmillan.

Gorecki, Paul 1995a. 'The Employment/Unemployment Position in Northern Ireland'. Paper presented at the Call Seminar, University of Ulster at Jordanstown, 3 May 1995. (To appear in the *First Trust Bank Review*.)

— 1995b. 'Peace and Political Stability: All-Ireland Implications'. In *The Two Economies of Ireland*, J. Bradley (ed.), Dublin: Oak Tree Press.

Gudgin, Graham and Geraldine O'Shea 1992. 'Avoiding the Worst: Northern Ireland in Recession'. *The Irish Banking Review*, Winter, 17-32.

— 1993. *Unemployment Forever? The Northern Ireland Economy in Recession and Beyond*. Belfast: The Northern Ireland Economic Research Centre.

Gudgin, Graham, Ronnie Scott, Eric Hanvey and Mark Hart 1995. 'The Role of Small Firms in Employment Growth, North and South'. In *The Two Economies of Ireland*. J. Bradley (ed.), Dublin: Oak Tree Press.

Gudgin, Graham 1995. 'Northern Ireland after the ceasefire'. *Irish Banking Review*, Autumn, 1-14.

Hall, R. 1962. *Report of the Joint Working Party on the Economy of Northern Ireland*. Cmnd 446, London: HMSO, October.

Hamilton, Douglas 1995. 'Peripherality, Development and the Political Economy of Northern Ireland'. In *Development Ireland — Contempory Issues*. P. Shirlow (ed.), London: Pluto Press.

— 1995. 'Inward Investment in Ireland'. In *Border Crossings*. Michael D'Arcy and Tim Dickson (eds.), Dublin: Gill and Macmillan.

Harris, Richard 1989. *The Growth and Structure of the UK Regional Economy 1963-85*. Aldershot: Avebury (Gower Publishing).

— 1991. *Regional Economic Policy in Northern Ireland 1945-1988*. Aldershot: Avebury (Gower Publishing).

Harris, Richard, Clifford Jefferson and John Spenser 1990. *The Northern Ireland Economy: A Comparative Study in the Economic Development of a Peripheral Region*. London: Longman.

Hirschman, A.O. 1958. *Exit, Voice and Loyalty: Responses to Decline in Firms, Organizations and States*. Cambridge: Harvard University Press.

Honohan, P. 1984. 'The Evolution of the Rate of Unemployment in Ireland 1962-83'. *Quarterly Economic Commentary*. The Economic and Social Research Institute, Dublin.

— 1992. 'The Link Between Irish and UK Unemployment'. *Quarterly Economic Commentary*. Spring. The Economic and Social Research Institute.

Hutton, Will 1994. *Britain and Northern Ireland, The State We're In — Failure and Opportunity*. Sir Charles Carter Lecture. Belfast: The Northern Ireland Economic Council.

— 1995. *The State We're In*. London: Jonathan Cape.

Jacquemin, Alexis and David Wright (eds) 1993. *The European Challenges Post 1992 Shaping Factors, Shaping Actors*. Aldershot: Edward Elgar.

Jefferson, Clifford 1990. 'The Labour Market'. In *The Northern Ireland Economy*. R. Harris, C. Jefferson and J. Spencer (eds.), London: Longmans.

Johnson, David S. and Liam Kennedy 1991. 'Nationalist historiography and the decline of the Irish economy: George O'Brien revisited'. In *Ireland's Histories:*

Aspects of State, Society and Ideology. S. Hutton and P. Stewart (eds.), London: Routledge.

Journal of the Statistical and Social Inquiry Society of Ireland, 1992. 'Symposium on the Findings of the Industrial Policy Review Group', 153-211.

Kearney, B. (ed.) 1995. *What Price CAP? Issues and Challenges Facing Agricultural and Rural Policy in the European Union.* Dublin: Institute of European Affairs.

Kennedy, K.A., T. Giblin and D. McHugh 1988. *The Economic Development of Ireland in the Twentieth Century.* London: Routledge.

Kennedy, K.A. 1993. *The Unemployment Crisis in Ireland.* Cork: Cork University Press.

Kenwood, A.G. and A.L. Lougheed 1992. *The Growth of the International Economy 1820-1990.* London: Routledge.

Keynes, J.M. 1933. 'National Self-Sufficiency'. *Studies* 22, 177-193.

KPMG Consultants 1995. *Social and Economic Consequences of Peace and Economic Reconstruction.* Report prepared by KPMG Management Consulting for the Forum for Peace and Reconciliation. Dublin: Stationery Office, June.

Krugman, Paul 1990. *The Age of Diminished Expectations.* Cambridge Massachusetts: The MIT Press.

— 1991. *Geography and Trade.* Cambridge Massachusetts: The MIT Press.

— 1992. 'Lessons of Massachusetts for EMU'. Paper presented at the Banco de Portugal conference on The Transition to EMU, Estoril, Portugal, 16-18 January.

— 1994. *Peddling Prosperity: Economic Sense and Nonsense in the Age of Diminished Expectations.* New York: W.W. Norton & Company.

Layard, R., S. Nickell and R. Jackman 1991. *Unemployment: Macroeconomic Performance and the Labour Market.* Oxford: Oxford University Press.

Lee, Joseph 1989. *Ireland 1912-1985: Politics and Society.* Cambridge (UK): Cambridge University Press.

Matthew, R.H. 1963. *The Belfast Regional Survey and Plan.* Cmnd 451, London: HMSO.

McAleese, Dermot 1985. 'American investment in Ireland'. In *Irish Studies 4: The Irish in America.* P.J. Drudy (ed.), 329-351, Cambridge (UK): Cambridge University Press.

McAleese, Dermot and Michael Counahan 1979: ' "Stickers" or "Snatchers": Employment in multi-national corporations during the recession'. *Oxford Bulletin of Economics and Statistics*, November.

McGarry, John and Brendan O'Leary 1995. *Explaining Northern Ireland: Broken Images.* Oxford: Blackwell Publishers Ltd.

179

McGregor, Peter, Kim Swales and Ya Ping Ying 1995. 'Regional Public-Sector and Current-Account Deficits: Do They Matter?' In *The Two Economies of Ireland: Public Policy, Growth and Employment.* J. Bradley (ed.), Dublin: Oak Tree Press.

McNally, Noel 1995. 'Strategic Planning Issues in Northern Ireland'. Paper presented at the conference on Regional Development: An All Ireland Perspective. Regional Studies Association (Irish Branch), St. Patrick's College, Maynooth, 14-15 September.

Mjoset, L. 1992. *The Irish Economy in a Comparative Institutional Perspective.* NESC Report No. 93, Dublin: The Stationery Office.

Molloy, Shane 1995. 'Lever Brothers: The Reality of a Single Market'. In *Border Crossings, Developing Ireland's Island Economy.* M. D'Arcy and T. Dickson (eds), Dublin: Gill and Macmillan.

Moore, B. and J. Rhodes 1973. 'Evaluating the Effects of British Regional Economic Policy'. *Economic Journal.* Vol. 83, no. 329, 87-110.

Munck, Ronnie 1993. *The Irish Economy: Results and Prospects.* London: Pluto Press.

Munck, Ronnie and Douglas Hamilton 1993. 'Alternative Scenarios'. In *The Irish Economy: Results and Prospects.* London: Pluto Press.

Murphy, Anthony and David Armstrong 1994. *A Picture of Catholic and Protestant Unemployed.* Belfast: CCRU.

National Economic and Social Council 1992. *The Association Between Economic Growth and Employment Growth in Ireland.* Report No. 94, Dublin: National Economic and Social Council.

— 1995. 'The Determinants of Competitive Advantage in Selected Irish Sectors'. Mimeo, Dublin: National Economic and Social Council.

Newell, A. and J. Symons 1990. 'The Causes of Ireland's Unemployment'. *The Economic & Social Review.* 21, 409-429.

Northern Ireland Economic Council 1990. *The Private Sector in the Northern Ireland Economy.* Report 82, Belfast: Northern Ireland Economic Development Office.

— 1991. *Economic Strategy in Northern Ireland.* Report 88, Belfast: Northern Ireland Economic Development Office.

— 1992. *Inward Investment in Northern Ireland.* Belfast: Northern Ireland Economic Development Office.

— 1993. *Northern Ireland and the Recent Recession: Cyclical Strength or Structural Weakness.* Belfast: Northern Ireland Economic Development Office.

— 1994. *The Implications of Peripherality for Northern Ireland.* Belfast: Northern Ireland Development Office.

— 1995. *The Economic Implications of Peace and Political Stability for Northern Ireland*. Occasional Paper 4. Belfast: Northern Ireland Development Office.

— 1995. 'The Implications of Peace and Political Stability in Northern Ireland for Selected Sectors: Inward Investment, Tourism and Security'. A Supplementary Paper to Council Occasional Paper 4. Belfast: Northern Ireland Development Office, June 1995.

Northern Ireland Economic Research Centre 1990. *The Northern Ireland Economy: Review and Forecasts to 1985*. Belfast: Northern Ireland Economic Research Centre.

Northern Ireland Growth Challenge 1995a. *Northern Ireland Growth Challenge: Interim Summary of Progress*. Belfast, May 1995.

— 1995b. *Cluster Strategies for Northern Ireland: An Interim Summary*. Belfast: The Northern Ireland Growth Challenge.

Northern Ireland Office 1994. *Structural Funds Plan for Northern Ireland*. Belfast: Northern Ireland Office.

O'Brien, George 1918. *The Economic History of Ireland in the Eighteenth Century*. Dublin and London: Maunsel.

— 1921. *The Economic History of Ireland from the Union to the Famine*. London: Longmans.

O'Connell, Phillip and Maureen Lyons 1994. 'Schemes for Success? Individual Characteristics and the Effects of Active Labour Market Programmes on Employment in Ireland: A Preliminary Analysis'. Mimeo, The Economic and Social Research Institute.

O'Connor, Fionnuala 1993. *In Search of a State: Catholics in Northern Ireland*. Belfast: The Blackstaff Press.

O'Donnell, Rory and Paul Teague 1993. 'The Potential and Limits to North-South Economic Co-operation'. In *The Economy of Northern Ireland*. P. Teague (ed.), London: Lawrence & Wishart.

O'Donnell, Rory 1995. 'Modernization and Social Partnership'. In *New Thinking for New Times*. Belfast: Democratic Dialogue, Issue No. 1, August.

OECD 1993. *Education at a Glance*. Paris: Organization for Economic Cooperation and Development.

Ó Gráda, Cormac 1994. *Ireland: A New Economic History 1780-1939*. Oxford: Clarendon Press.

Ó Gráda, Cormac and Brendan Walsh 1995. 'Fertility and Population in Ireland, North and South'. *Population Studies*. 49, 259-279.

Ohmae, Kenichi 1994. 'The Rise of the Region State'. *Foreign Affairs*, 78-87.

181

—, ed. 1995. 'Putting Global Logic First'. In *The Evolving Global Economy*. Harvard: Harvard Business Review Books, 129-137.

O'Leary, Brendan, Tom Lyne, Jim Marshall and Bob Rowthorn 1993. *Northern Ireland: Sharing Authority*. London: Institute for Public Policy Research.

O'Leary, Brendan and John McGarry 1995. *Explaining Northern Ireland: Broken Images*. Oxford: Basil Blackwell.

O'Malley, Eoin 1989. *Industry and Economic Development: The Challenge for the Latecomer*. Dublin: Gill and Macmillan.

— 1993. *An Analysis of Secondary Employment Associated With Manufacturing Industry*. General Research Series, Paper No. 167. Dublin: The Economic and Social Research Institute.

O'Rourke, Kevin 1994. 'Industrial Policy, Employment Policy and the Nontraded Sector'. Barrington Prize Lecture. Presented to the Statistical and Social Inquiry Society of Ireland, 24 November.

Porter, Michael P. 1990. *The Competitive Advantage of Nations*. London: Macmillan.

Quigley, W.G.H. 1976. *Economic and Industrial Strategy for Northern Ireland: Report by Review Team*. Belfast: HMSO.

— 1992. *Ireland — An Island Economy*. Paper presented at the Annual Conference of the Confederation of Irish Industry. Dublin, 28 February.

— 1992. *Northern Ireland: A Decade for Decision*. Annual Sir Charles Carter Lecture. Report 95, Belfast: Northern Ireland Economic Development Office.

— 1995. 'Introductory Remarks'. In *The Two Economies of Ireland*. J. Bradley (ed.), Dublin: The Oak Tree Press.

Regional Development Centre (RDC) 1994. *Cross Border Technology and Innovation Project: Initial Report*. Dundalk: Newry/Dundalk Technology Group.

Reich, Robert 1993. *The Work of Nations: A Blueprint for the Future*. London: Simon and Schuster.

Roche, Patrick J. and J. Esmond Birnie 1995. *An Economics Lesson for Irish Nationalists and Republicans*. Belfast: Ulster Unionist Information Institute.

Roper, Stephen and Andrew Schofield 1990. 'NIMOD - An Econometric Model of Northern Ireland'. Mimeo, Northern Ireland Economic Research Centre, February.

Roper, Stephen and Geraldine O'Shea 1991. 'The Effect of Labour Subsidies in Northern Ireland 1967-79: A Simulation Analysis'. *Scottish Journal of Political Economy* 38, No. 3, 273-292.

Roper, Stephen and Graham Gudgin 1991. *Economic Forecasts for Northern Ireland 1991-2000*. Belfast: Northern Ireland Economic Research Centre.

Rowthorn, Bob 1987. 'Northern Ireland: An Economy in Crisis'. In P. Teague (ed.), *Beyond the Rhetoric*. London: Lawrence & Wishart.

Rowthorn, Bob and N. Wayne 1988. *Northern Ireland: The Political Economy of Conflict*. Oxford: The Polity Press.

Sabel, Charles F. 1989. 'Flexible Specialization and the Re-emergence of Regional Economies'. In *Reversing Industrial Decline*. Paul Hirst and Jonathan Zeitlin (eds.), Oxford: Berg Publishers Limited.

Scott, Ronnie and Maureen O'Reilly 1992. *Exports of Northern Ireland Manufacturing Companies 1990*. Belfast: Northern Ireland Economic Research Centre.

Share, Bernard 1992. *Shannon Departures: A Study in Regional Initiatives*. Dublin: Gill and Macmillan.

Sheehan, Maura 1993. 'Government Financial Assistance and Manufacturing Investment in Northern Ireland'. *Regional Studies*. Vol. 27, No. 6, 527-540.

Smyth, Austin 1995. 'Transport: A Hard Road Ahead'. In *Border Crossings, Developing Ireland's Island Economy*. M. D'Arcy and T. Dickson (eds.), Dublin: Gill and Macmillan.

Smyth, Michael 1993. 'The Public Sector in the Economy'. In *The Economy of Northern Ireland*, P. Teague (ed.), London: Lawrence & Wishart.

Stationery Office 1958. *Economic Development*, Dublin: The Stationery Office, Pr 4803.

— 1983a. *A Comparative Description of the Economic Structure and Situation*. North and South, New Ireland Forum, Dublin: The Stationery Office.

— 1983b. *The Cost of Violence arising from the Northern Ireland Crisis since 1969*. New Ireland Forum, Dublin: The Stationery Office.

— 1984. *The Macroeconomic Consequences of Integrated Economic Policy, Planning and Coordination in Ireland*. Report prepared by DKM Consultants for the New Ireland Forum, Dublin: The Stationery Office.

— 1985. *The Economic Consequences of the Division of Ireland Since 1920*. New Ireland Forum, Dublin: The Stationery Office.

— 1992. *A Time for Change: Industrial Policy for the 1990s*. Report of the Industrial Policy Review Group (Culliton Report), Dublin: The Stationery Office.

— 1993. *Ireland: National Development Plan 1994-1999*. Pn. 0222, Dublin: The Stationery Office.

Tansey, Paul 1995. 'Tourism: A Product with Big Potential'. In *Border Crossings, Developing Ireland's Island Economy*. M. D'Arcy and T. Dickson (eds). Dublin: Gill and Macmillan.

Teague, P. 1987. *Beyond the Rhetoric: Politics, the Economy and Social Policy in Northern Ireland*. London: Lawrence and Wishart.

Teague, P. (ed.) 1993. *The Economy of Northern Ireland: Perspectives for Structural Change*, London: Lawrence and Wishart.

Teague, P. and John McCartney 1995. 'Big Differences that Matter: Labour Market Systems in Ireland, North and South'. In *The Two Economies of Ireland*. J. Bradley (ed.), Dublin: Oak Tree Press.

Thomsen, Stephen and Stephen Woolcock 1993. *Direct Investment and European Integration: Competition among Firms and Governments*. London: The Royal Institute of International Affairs and Pinter Publishers.

Tomlinson, Mike 1994. *25 Years On: The Costs of War and the Dividends of Peace*. The Second Annual Frank Cahill Memorial Lecture. Belfast: West Belfast Economic Forum.

Walsh, James A. 1995. *Regions in Ireland: A Statistical Profile*. Dublin: The Regional Studies Association (Irish Branch.)

Whyte, John 1990. *Interpreting Northern Ireland*. Oxford: Clarendon Press.

Wijkman, Per 1990. 'Patterns of Production and Trade'. In W. Wallace (ed.), *The Dynamics of European Integration*, London: Pinter Publishers.

Wilson R. 1996. 'Asking the Right Question'. In *Reconstituting Politics*, Report No. 3, Belfast: Democratic Dialogue.

Notes

Chapter One — Introduction

1. The IRA announced a 'complete cessation of military operations' from midnight, 31 August 1994. The Combined Loyalist Military Command announced a ceasefire from midnight, 13 October.
2. We use the terms 'North' in our study to denote Northern Ireland and 'South' to denote the Republic of Ireland, since to do otherwise would be very cumbersome. Since North and South are frequently juxtaposed in the context of the island of Ireland, little ambiguity is likely to arise from this compact, convenient, if somewhat imprecise nomenclature. The term 'Ireland' is sometimes used as a synonym for the island of Ireland, and after 1922 always in its geographical sense. The term 'troubles', widely used in the North to describe the civil unrest and violence that broke out after 1968, is also used throughout our report.
3. The term 'cohesion' is used in the EU context to denote convergence of standards of living, as measured, say, by real income (GDP) per capita. The term 'convergence' is used to denote adherence to the Maastricht criteria of inflation, interest rates, borrowing, debt, etc.
4. There is considerable debate, for example, on how important political factors like the MacBride Principles were in deterring American investors from the North (Bardon 1992, 799). Any negative impact would tend to be compounded with more direct troubles effects.
5. The Public Capital Programme, which had contracted sharply during most of the 1980s, began to grow again from the early 1990s. The domestic co-financing requirement of the Delors I and II Community Support Frameworks (or Structural Funds) was one reason for increased public expenditure on the capital side.
6. For example, see McGarry and O'Leary (1995, ch. 7) for a stylish and effective demolition job on purely economic explanations of the causes and cures of the Northern troubles.
7. A recently published study by Cormac Ó Gráda covers the period 1780-1939 and gives central place to economic developments in a wide-sweeping interpretation of Irish history (Ó Gráda 1994). Jonathan Bardon's *A History of Ulster* also integrates economic aspects into his historical narrative (Bardon 1992). On the other hand, Joseph Lee's highly critical analysis of the 'failure' of Southern

development in the twentieth century can be criticized for its limited and possibly inappropriate international comparisons together with its anachronistic economic perspective (Lee 1989).

8. Key 'nationalist' economic studies of Irish history are those of George O'Brien (1918 and 1921). Johnson and Kennedy (1991) provides a concise critical re-evaluation. Nevertheless, the thesis that Ireland's economic ills are overwhelmingly of British origin continues to have its adherents (Adams 1995, 181-182).

9. In his Barrington Prize lecture, O'Rourke asserts the alternative view that the non-traded sector (mainly services) is in no sense derivative; rather, its health is the key to competitiveness and overdue structural reforms could generate large welfare gains (O'Rourke 1994). Recent liberalization in the area of access transport to the island has shown that the private sector does respond to deregulation incentives and improved physical infrastructure.

CHAPTER TWO — THE ORIGINS OF THE TWO ECONOMIES, 1750-1960

1. A related theme originates from the Marxist interpretative tradition, suggesting that Ireland's economic link with British capitalism has on occasion and in some sectors been malign (Munck 1993, chs 1 and 2). The late Raymond Crotty further develops the interpretation of Ireland as an example of capitalist colonization (Crotty 1986).

2. A national system of innovation is defined by Mjoset as encompassing the institutions and economic structures which affect the rate and direction of innovative activities in the economy (Mjoset 1992, 43-50).

3. The concepts of 'exit' and 'voice' were first used by Albert Hirschman. They develop the idea that there is a wide range of economic processes for the efficient unfolding of which both individual, economic action (via exit) and participatory, political action (via voice) have important constructive roles to play. These concepts widen the notion of market failure and their application illuminates many important economic and political processes (Hirschman 1970).

4. A fascinating insight into the tensions in the world economy between maintaining policies of laissez faire or retreating behind protectionism in the early 1930s is provided by Keynes' Finlay lecture, delivered at University College Dublin in 1932 (Keynes 1933).

5. Ó Gráda points out that the proto-industrial zone of the North and North-West was an area of poor land and small farms, where the textile industry bulked large (Ó Gráda 1994, 32-42).

6. For example, the Yorkshireman Edward Harland relied on the help of a Liverpool-German financier and the German Gustav Wolff to set up Harland and Wolff (Ó Gráda 1994, 324-331).

7. Jonathan Bardon's *Belfast: An Illustrated History*, provides a fascinating account of the political, social and economic aspects of the rise of linen and shipbuilding in the mid and late nineteenth century north-east region (Bardon 1982).

8. Mjoset (1992) is a seminal study of Southern economic underperformance that draws carefully from a wide European literature on social and economic development. Lee (1989) is a more discursive historical narrative.

9. See Keynes (1933) for the reflections of an economist of world stature on free trade and protection. Kenwood and Lougheed (1992) analyses the impact of World War I on the workings of the international economy and its subsequent collapse during the 1930s.

10. The sectors are indicated as follows: (1) Textiles; (2) Grain milling; (3) Brewing and malting; (4) Iron, steel, ships and vehicles; (5) Clothing, millinery; (6) Butter, cheese; (7) Bacon curing; (8) Bread and biscuits; (9) Distilling; (10) Printing and publishing. In sectors (3) and (7) the method used indicated Southern shares greater than 100 per cent, so an upper bound was imposed (Ó Gráda 1994, 312-313).

CHAPTER THREE — THE TWO ECONOMIES DURING THE TROUBLES: 1960-94

1. North-South comparisons, if and when they are carried out, are not always value-free exercises. A recent interpretation of Southern performance from a unionist stand-point is contained in Roche and Birnie (1995). Northern economic performance does not loom so large in the concerns of Southern economists, who are more preoccupied with the wider world economy, and the key role played by the British economy. The writings of the Sinn Féin leader, Gerry Adams, tend to be equally damning of the economic performance of North and South (e.g., Adams 1995).

2. None of the first four published ESRI Medium-Term Reviews of 1986,1987,1989 and 1991 made any reference at all to Northern Ireland. The most recent 1994 Review refers briefly to the Mezzogiorno-like dependency problem in the North. The NIERC medium-term forecasts for Northern Ireland refer only in passing to comparative North-South performance, and then mainly in the area of demographic trends (Roper and Gudgin 1991; Gudgin and O'Shea 1993).

3. A more recent NIEC study of Northern peripherality also makes few references to the similar problems of the South (NIEC 1994). Indeed, it is a tragedy that such studies are still carried out, North and South, in almost complete isolation from each other.

4. Northern and Southern economic models are unique in the EU in that they contain explicit migration mechanisms, reflecting the strength and importance of this link, mainly to the British labour market (e.g., Bradley, Whelan and Wright 1993; Roper and Schofield 1990).

5. The relatively strong performance of Northern indigenous industry over the past five years may owe much to the role of the subvention in stimulating demand for non-traded goods rather than to any major improvement in underlying productivity or competitiveness. The role of small firms, North and South, is examined in Gudgin et al. (1995).

6. A unique early joint North-South economic analysis is Gibson and Spencer, 1975, which contains an outline of a simple formalized Keynesian model schema of the two regions. The only other study known to us is the HERMIN and NIMIN North-South modelling exercise, described in Bradley and Wright (1992) and Bradley, Whelan and Wright (1993). Both regions have, of course, been extensively analysed and modelled in isolation from each other (see Appendix).

7. The recent study of the UK regional economies by Harris (1989), excluded any mention of, or comparison with, the Republic of Ireland and even ignored links between individual UK regions and the rest of the UK and the external world.

8. Transfer pricing arises when foreign firms based in the South understate the price of their imported intermediate inputs, both materials and R&D, and thus overstate the extent of added value arising in their Irish subsidiary. Increased profits arise from the low rate of Southern corporation tax in manufacturing (10 per cent), and these profits are then mainly repatriated or otherwise used outside of Ireland.

9. An early analysis of the costs of violence is provided in *The Cost of Violence arising from the Northern Ireland Crisis since 1969* (Stationery Office 1983b). A more recent analysis is available in DKM (1994).

10. A product has a high income elasticity of demand when a 1 per cent increase in consumers' income generates an increased response in demand for the product of significantly greater than one. The phenomenal growth in sales of microcomputers is indicative of high demand elasticities. Many standard food and textile products typically have demand elasticities lower than unity.

11. The Dublin-based International Financial Services Centre (IFSC) is an example of a market service activity directed almost exclusively at world markets.

12. This is an area where further research is needed, and is hampered by the absence of up-to-date Northern input-output matrices, tools that permit analysis of inter-sectoral linkages and dependencies.

13. Tourism expenditures have high multipliers in the sense that tourists tend to purchase home produced goods and services such as food, drink, entertainment, holiday accommodation, transport, etc. On the other hand, a unit of manufactured exports tends to be associated directly with quite high imports of raw materials and intermediate goods, and thus has a lower multiplier effect on the domestic economy.

14. For a detailed analysis of Northern security expenditure, see KPMG Consultants (1995, 39-56).

15. The Mezzogiorno region of southern Italy has given its name to a phenomenon that arose when the much richer northern Italian regions gave long-term income transfers to the South, one of whose side effects was to lock the South into a low efficiency, low productivity, low entrepreneurial dependency (CEC 1993).

16. Care must be taken in comparing unemployment rates, both between countries and over time. For the South we use the measure based on the Labour Force Survey, which is a few percentage points lower than the entitlements-based Live Register measure, since the former captures more accurately the concept of active job-search. The UK measures are roughly equivalent to the LFS.

17. Annual net migration flows for the years 1990-94 were as follows (in thousands, where a negative sign indicated a net inward flow): 22.9, 2.0, -2.0, 6.0, and 10.0. With the exception of the year 1990, these flows are low by historical standards.
18. Ó Gráda and Walsh (1995), touch on another aspect of emigration from the North, namely the traditionally higher rate of emigration by Catholics compared to that of other religious groups, and the reversal of this pattern in the period 1971-91 (pp. 273-274).
19. The polar case of this argument is presented in Honohan (1984 and 1992). In his 1984 paper it was argued, using data from 1962-83, that the unemployment rate in the South tended to remain at about 5 percentage points above the UK level and that any shift in Southern and British unemployment rates away from the long-run equilibrium would induce migration flows that restore the equilibrium differential. The true position is probably a lot more complex.
20. One would expect, of course, to get greater variation in unemployment rates the smaller the regions/areas analysed.
21. The regional subdivisions shown are abbreviations of Ballymena, Belfast, Coleraine and Craigavon (all east of the Bann), and Cookstown, Dungannon, Enniskillen, Derry, Magherafelt, Newry, Omagh and Strabane (all west of the Bann). The data source is Jefferson (1990).
22. The regional subdivisions shown in the graph indicate Dublin, Mid East, South East, South West, Mid West, West, Border and Midlands. The source is Walsh (1995).
23. Issues relating to regional concentration and agglomeration effects will be taken up in chapter 5 below.
24. The fact that supporting Northern Ireland had become a burden on the British taxpayer is expressed most stridently in Rowthorn and Wayne (1988), who go as far as using the term 'work-house' economy. However, what limited data are available indicate that Scotland and Wales are also in receipt of net transfers from London, albeit smaller ones on a per capita basis than in the case of the North (Blake 1995).
25. In a recent study of the Northern public sector, Smyth (1993) has stated that: 'Expansion of the public sector of Northern Ireland has been a surrogate for autonomous growth, a buttress against political instability and remains the dominant feature of the region's economy.'
26. The Northern estimates are based on an approximate attribution of UK indirect taxes to Northern Ireland, and assume that receipts are confined to revenue and other receipts generated from the North's own economic activity (Bradley 1990). No account is taken of the return to Britain in terms of increased sales to the North arising from the subvention.
27. In an expansionary fiscal contraction (EFC), public expenditure cuts will reduce the need for future high taxes. This will be foreseen by rational, optimizing agents in the private sector who will immediately increase their consumption, possibly more than offsetting the contractionary effects of the cuts.
28. Bradley and Whelan (1995) incorporated forward looking, or rational, expectations into a Southern macro-model (HERMIN) and found that the strong performance of private consumption could not be accounted for convincingly by expectational effects related to personal income and consumption. Rather, they suggest that it could very easily be explained by the

unexpectedly strong growth in the world economy, particularly in Britain (the 'Lawson' boom), which occurred at the same time.

29. It should be noted that neither public consumption nor public investment contracted seriously during the post Lawson recession. The analysis of Gudgin and O'Shea (1993) appears to have been formulated purely in terms of private consumption.

30. In Figure 3.13 the Northern trade balance data for 1961-74 are taken directly from the publication *The Trade of Northern Ireland*, published by the Dept. of Commerce. After the publication of Northern trade data ended in 1974, the figures are estimated residually from the output-expenditure identity and are only rough approximations. The exact details are available from the author.

31. The terminology here needs to be slightly pedantic. Sales of Northern goods and services to Britain are termed 'external' sales. Sales of the same goods to the South, or to other destinations outside Britain, are termed 'exports'.

32. The narrowness of the Northern export base is illustrated by the fact that a small number of major exporters were responsible for a large proportion of all exports: the three largest exporting firms accounted for 40 per cent of all exports and the ten largest for 54 per cent.

33. It would be interesting to estimate how much of this Southern trade surplus with the North arises out of the North's subvention from Britain. Any reduction of the subvention could have serious consequences for Southern firms.

34. We return to the issues involved in evaluating potential gains from increased North-South trade later in chapter 6.

35. Sophisticated computer models are sometimes used to lend credence to this type of hypothetical scenario analysis. Simpler approaches can also be used, based on very crude assumptions. No analysis of the Northern troubles has yet been carried out using computer models of the economy.

CHAPTER FOUR — ECONOMIC POLICY STRUCTURES ON THE ISLAND

1. Bradley and Whelan (1992) give an account of the historic link between the Southern currency and sterling, the reasons for terminating it, and the economic consequences of the South joining the EMS narrow band in the absence of the UK.

2. The difficulties being experienced at present within the European Union as it attempts to move forward from the Single Market to Economic and Monetary Union (EMU) illustrates the intimate relationship between elements of economic policy and political sovereignty, particularly when the former is seen to threaten the latter.

3. We use the terms nationalist and unionist in the following paragraphs as if they each represented homogeneous groups with common views. Clearly this is not the case, and a wide diversity of attitudes to the economy exists within each such grouping.

. Opinion polls in the North indicate that the majority of nationalists seem unwilling to accept a lower standard of living as the price of closer North-South political links. One expects that polls in the South would equally show a reluctance to pay even a modest price in terms of higher taxes to support a higher Northern standard of living. The forces of Mammon appear to dominate the forces of nationalism on both sides of the border!

. If, on the other hand, the North were to become a dynamic innovative region within the UK, making a tax contribution substantially greater than its public expenditure, it seems unlikely that either unionist or nationalist attitudes to the South would differ from the case where the North requires subvention funding to maintain its higher standard of living.

. The book by Lyne, Marshall and Rowthorn (1993) provides detailed examples of possible political-institutional arrangements between Britain and the South, together with their implications for the public finances of both countries.

. In fact, the only economic factor taken into account by O'Leary et al. (1993) is the size of the Northern subvention and the impossibility of financing it under the options of Irish unification or Northern independence.

. This comment is not intended as a criticism of the Forum report prepared by DKM (Stationery Office 1984). The brief given to the consultants did not emphasize wider economic policy and performance issues.

. More formally, in the South the public expenditure multipliers are much smaller than in economies such as the UK, Germany and the US, due to the openness of the Southern economy and the leakage of demand abroad through increased imports. These multipliers are further reduced if any public expenditure increase must be financed by offsetting tax rises. Bradley, Whelan and Wright (1993) illustrate this process quantitatively using the Southern HERMIN macroeconomic model.

0. For example, the extraordinary strength of sterling in the years immediately after the election of the Conservative Government in 1979 must have damaged the Northern economy at least as much as it damaged the British economy (Hutton 1994 and 1995).

1. British-Irish policy cooperation over the Common Travel Area, with consequential cooperation in regard to animal and plant health, derived more from the original Government of Ireland Act of 1920 than from any more recent dynamic policy cooperation process. Furthermore, the Anglo-Irish Free Trade Agreement of 1965 was a response to the development of free trade in the EEC and, in particular, to the opening of the British market to the EFTA countries. Many other areas of political-economic cooperation (such as similarity of legislation, joint British-Irish organization of various professions, cooperation on maritime matters, etc.) could also be held to owe their existence to the strength of the pre-1920 Union rather than from any more recent Anglo-Irish policy dynamic.

2. Examples of similarities between the South and Britain that carried over from the previous Union include a broadly similar legal system — which has only slowly diverged as reform proceeds at different paces in both jurisdictions — and the common organization of many professions.

13. The case against closer formal policy cooperation between North and South has been put strongly in Roche and Birnie (1995), and in a series of Cadogan Group pamphlets (Cadogan Group 1992, 1994 and 1995). We return to these matters in chapter 6 below.

14. The use of the term 'single island economy' by Sir George Quigley in his CII address should probably be thought of as a case of 'coordinated development' in our terms (Quigley 1992).

15. Thus, the British perception is that the South 'broke' the link with sterling in 1979 and that any disruptive currency movements between the Irish pound and sterling are the South's own fault. The Southern perception would be that the Irish pound entered into a formalized EU currency harmonization, together with most of the larger and stronger EU member States, and that the UK opted out. Unfortunately, the high, if declining, trade links between the South and the UK make this more than a semantic issue.

16. A similar process of devolution might occur in other UK regions, such as Scotland and Wales. However, geography and history make it very unlikely that the South (of Ireland) would have any role in these aspects of British devolution.

17. The 'maximalist' and 'minimalist' cooperation cases of O'Donnell and Teague (1993) are the closest to our polar cases of 'separate economic development' and 'single island economy'. Munck and Hamilton explore a series of different political-economic scenarios for the island of Ireland, ranging from a continuation of Direct Rule for the North to the reunification of Ireland within a radical democratic framework (Munck and Hamilton 1993).

18. The KPMG study examines other aspects of the North-South policy coordination issue: displacement of foreign direct investment from South to North (pp. 62-64); revaluation of the Irish pound against sterling (p. 64); different performance responses of the border regions (pp. 65-66); and different reallocations of security savings, North and South (pp. 67-68).

CHAPTER FIVE — THE WIDER SOCIO-ECONOMIC CONTEXT FOR THE ISLAND

1. The Mezzogiorno region of Southern Italy has given its name to a type of dependency that can arise when the wealthy regions of a country attempt to subvent the poorer regions through income transfers (CEC 1993).

2. For an accessible and readable account of the recent debate on economic policy-making in the US, see Paul Krugman's two recent books, *The Age of Diminished Expectations* and *Peddling Prosperity* (1990 and 1994). Will Hutton's recent bestseller, *The State We're In*, (Hutton 1995) is a polemic account of the debate in the UK.

3. The coordination role for public policy is well illustrated in the case of Japan, a large economy, where it operates through the Ministry of International Trade and Industry (MITI) in association with the *Keidanren*, Japan's employers' organization, and the *Keiretsus*, the large business conglomerates (Best 1990, 167-202).

The Culliton Report in the South makes no reference to the North (Stationery Office 1992). Nor do Northern documents like *Competing in the 1990s* or *Growing Competitively — A Review of Economic Development Policy in Northern Ireland*, prepared by the DED, make any reference to the South (DED 1990 and 1995). The analysis and action plan associated with the Northern Ireland Growth Challenge envisages no explicit Southern cooperation, although it does reference Southern success as examples that may be of relevance to the North (NIGC, 1995a and 1995b).

Joint North-South guides on domestic trade and import substitution possibilities have been drawn up by An Bord Tráchtála (in the South) and the IDB in the North. North-South joint tourism promotion are in progress; IBEC (in the South) and the CBI(NI) (in the North) operate a Joint Council and joint committees whose role is to encourage collaboration of Northern and Southern firms.

FitzGerald (1995) explores Southern demographic issues and their policy implications. Compton (1995) examines the situation in the North. Ó Gráda and Walsh (1995) compare Northern and Southern demographic factors. Bradley et al. (1995) explores North-South issues in human capital. Teague and McCarthy (1995) provides an overview of North-South labour market institutional issues.

'Dead-weight' is a term used by economists to describe the situation where a private agent (say, a firm) takes advantage of a subsidy to carry out an action that would have been undertaken even in the complete absence of the subsidy. For an evaluation of industrial policy in the South, see the Proceedings of a Symposium on the Findings of the Industrial Policy Review Group, (JSSISI 1992, 153-211). Harris (1991) and NIEC (1994) provide critical evaluations of the performance of Northern industrial policy.

Michael Enright, Professor Porter's associate at the Harvard Business School, was a consultant both to the Southern Industrial Policy Review Group (the Culliton committee) and to the Northern Ireland Growth Challenge.

The most systematic research available relates to the North (NIGC 1995a and 1995b). The NESC have research in progress on the Southern situation (NESC 1995). There appears to be no cross-referencing between the Northern and Southern projects.

10. Big Northern manufacturers, such as Desmonds and Moy Park, supply UK chain stores, such as Marks & Spencers and Sainsburys. This could lead to the type of supply-side links we are emphasizing, but has remained underdeveloped to date. Furthermore, these links are directed at consumers (final demand) rather than at other firms (intermediate demand).

11. The reader is referred to section 4.3.2 for a discussion of the more obvious cases where co-ordinated North-South policy planning would put in place the economic preconditions for deeper supply-side business linkages. The absence of such coordination would appear to be the main barrier to the natural development of such links since the political partition of the island.

12. It must be said, however, that the branch plants of the multinationals that locate in the South have not in general been characterized by 'footloose' behaviour (McAleese and Counahan 1979). Although they have developed limited linkages with the rest of the economy (O'Malley 1989,

177-181), they have displayed a long-term commitment to the country that is probably not unconnected with the fiscal and other advantages offered. The Northern situation was very different (Bardon 1992, 784-786).

13. For example, it would be inconceivable in the South to consider seriously a dysfunctional scenario where the private sector would 'go it alone' in the absence or against the flow of public policy initiatives. Yet such a hypothetical scenario is contemplated in the Northern Ireland Growth Challenge.

14. As shown by James Bradley et al. (1986), the area close to Belfast benefited during the 1950s and 1960s from an industrial policy that encouraged inward investment to locate near the Belfast growth pole. This served to protect 'inner' areas such as Antrim and towns such as Carrickfergus, but may have resulted in relative disadvantage to 'outer' towns such as Newry.

15. Today, it would be preferable to include a wide range of private support services with manufacturing since some of the distinctions between these sectors have vanished as a result of the 'hiving off' or 'unbundling' of services that were previously classified within manufacturing.

16. O'Malley (1989) develops the 'late-comer' thesis as an explanation of the poor Southern manufacturing performance since independence.

17. It could also be argued that the main incentive for attracting inward investment, i.e., the low corporate tax regime, was itself a major obstacle to linkage development within Ireland. The transfer pricing activity which it encourages is most easily operated where branch plants in Ireland maintain their major supply links with affiliate plants located abroad.

18. In the eighteenth and nineteenth centuries industries needed to cluster close to sources of energy (coal, water, etc.) and at transport hubs near large centres of population. However, in the latter part of the twentieth century the concept of geographical distance has been diluted and redefined by dramatic improvements and cost reductions in communications technologies.

19. The failure of Craigavon, a 'new' Northern town, to generate self-sustaining growth is an aspect of migrational difficulties within the North (Bardon 1992, 717).

20. The constancy of firm failure rates across regions is a widely experienced phenomenon. Hence, regional variation in employment creation comes from differences in firm formation rates (Baldwin and Gorecki 1990).

21. Location ratios measure how a region's share of total national employment in any sector compares with its share of national population. A score of unity implies that the region's employment and population shares are equal. A score of less than unity implies that the region has less of a share of national employment than it has of national population, i.e., that it has lost out in the regional allocation of employment.

22. At present the Southern agglomerations and clusters are of a rather weak variety and are quite unlike the dynamic clusters in regions like BadenWurttemberg in Germany, Silicon Valley and Route 128 in the US, and the M4 Corridor in the UK. Nevertheless, the levels of skills involved are being constantly upgraded and Ireland has become an attractive location for certain high-technology activities simply because of the presence of other similar industries, with their labour market externalities.

23. The low unemployment rates of the two cohesion countries Greece and Portugal are not shown in Figure 5.6 since there is considerable unrecorded unemployment in these countries due to their large agriculture sectors and lack of a well developed social welfare system (Bradley et al. 1995).
24. The most recent authoritative analysis of inter-community differences in unemployment patterns is Murphy and Armstrong (1994). For surveys of the debate on Northern unemployment and its relationship to discrimination, see Whyte 1990, 52-66 and O'Leary and McGarry 1995, 282-306.
25. The UK opt-out from the Social Chapter of the Maastricht Treaty has obvious implications for the evolution of labour costs North and South of the border. Low labour costs provide certain clear attractions to domestic producers and foreign investors, but few powerful and wealthy nations have built their success on this process alone (Porter 1990; Reich 1993). Indeed, it seems doubtful that the full UK opt-out would survive a change of government.

CHAPTER SIX — THE TWO ISLAND ECONOMIES: FUTURE DEVELOPMENT PATHS

1. Jacquemin and Wright (eds), (1993) is an example of long-range analysis coordinated by the European Commission. A recent publication by the Dutch Central Planning Bureau provides an example of state-of-the-art long-term scenario studies for the Netherlands, a country where economists like Jan Tinbergen pioneered quantitative analysis and planning before the second world war (Central Planning Bureau 1992).
2. It has been suggested that the impact of peace on the Northern economy could be quite minor, other than for public finance aspects (Gudgin 1995). If so, the pre-ceasefire Northern forecasts may retain some post ceasefire validity, at least to the extent that other assumptions (say about the world economy) have not changed.
3. Hutton (1995) documents the divisive social nature of some elements of British public policy during the 1980s.
4. Although UK citizenship implies equality of levels of public services such as education, health, pensions, welfare benefits, etc., it is conceivable that the subvention might be reduced as a matter of policy if security savings were not fully recycled within the North (Gudgin 1995, 12). This would be likely to deflate regional demand and induce recession in that element of the private sector that is not export oriented.
5. The North also receives Structural Funds and agricultural price support from the EU, through London. However, at least some elements of these EU transfers may already be factored into the British subvention to the North.
6. Objective 1 countries are those with a level of GDP per capita less than 75 per cent of the EU average whose general economic development lags behind the average. At present the Objective 1 regions include the whole of Greece, (the South of) Ireland and Portugal. Spain and Italy have

large regions designated as Objective 1, while Northern Ireland is an Objective 1 region of the UK (Bradley et al. 1995).

7. Although both North and South have high costs relative to many low cost Asian and Eastern European producers, Northern costs can be considerably lower than in the South. For example, the 1994 comparative construction cost indices for warehouses are as follows: the North is 75, the South is 117, with Britain at 100. The comparative indices for office construction are 75, 89 and 100, respectively.

8. A classic study of the 'British' problem prior to the supply-side reforms of the last decade is Bacon and Eltis (1976). Hutton (1994) concentrates on more recent problems.

9. Claims that the North was one of the fastest growing parts of the UK over the last quarter century (Gudgin 1995) are not quite as impressive when subjected to closer scrutiny. Not only was most of the employment growth concentrated in the public sector, but the knock-on effects of both the public sector and subvention-financed income transfers on the sheltered part of the private sector may have produced much of the remainder.

10. In defining the scenario for 'Peace and Political Agreement' (PPA), the KPMG report states: 'Under this scenario, it is assumed that there is decisive progress towards a political settlement within two to three years and, from an early stage, there is a perception that such a settlement will be reached. *This scenario makes no assumptions about the details of such a scenario.* The key assumption is that investment decisions in industry and tourism are taken without any associated risk-premium, as assumed to continue to apply under the ceasefire option.' (KPMG 1995, 14. Our italics.)

11. It should be noted that between 30 and 41 per cent of the private sector employment increase is classified as non-permanent, since it would vanish unless sustained by State funding.

12. The experience of Belfast in the second half of the nineteenth century, examined in chapter 2, provides some optimism for a late twentieth or early twenty first century emulation of that previous success. However, a very particular configuration of circumstances supported rapid growth in the north-east region of Ireland in the nineteenth century and it is difficult to see that these might be repeated today in the context of a British economy that is less vibrant or dynamic.

13. It is important to take the relative sizes of two trading regions into account in any comparisons of trade integration. A small nation like the South has a limited supply capacity and is never likely to appear as large in per capita sales into a major economy like, say, Britain.

14. The understandable remoteness of the relationships and contacts of Northern unionists with the South is paralleled by a more surprising remoteness between nationalists and the South (O'Connor, 1993). It is vital not to underestimate the social and economic benefits that could flow from closer North-South contacts between people in all walks of life.

15. An interesting account of the attitudes of a small sample of firms already operating on an all-island basis is provided in an appendix to D'Arcy and Dickson (1995). Not all aspects of North-South policy and institutional differences are seen as negative, and some firms display great ingenuity in getting the best of both worlds!

16. Economists use the more precise term 'Pareto-optimal', meaning that, under certain assumptions, a free-market economy will allocate resources in a way that makes it impossible to make somebody

better off without making somebody else worse off. This concept has been recently invoked as an argument against all-Ireland institutions (Roche and Birnie 1995, 38-39). To counter this argument one needs to discuss the problem of 'missing' markets and introduce the notion of an 'externality', which we develop later.

17. The massive intervention by the Southern Government in the economy during the late 1970s and early 1980s was justified in part in terms of a desire to abolish unemployment (a market failure). However the result was to lead to a destabilization of the economy, with huge increases in the public debt, increases in taxation and eventually severe cut-backs in public expenditure. Ultimately the policy intervention probably caused more unemployment than it cured (Barry and Bradley 1990).

18. For examples of policy areas where a failure to cooperate has imposed higher costs on the island, refer to section 4.3.2. The exact details of where cooperative policy structures should be set up, as well as how they should be structured, will require further targeted research in the context of specific political settlements on the island. These matters go beyond the remit of the present study.

19. For example, Toronto is essentially incorporated into a corridor which goes as far south as Detroit and Cleveland and manages to successfully span two separate jurisdictions.

20. For example, the area contained within the Belfast-Dublin Economic Corridor (at about 5,900 square miles, or 18 per cent of the total island) is smaller than the area of the State of Massachusetts (at about 8,500 square miles).

21. For example, Michael Best describes how the institution building that sustained the small-firm growth of the Third Italy originated with the post war reforms following the defeat of fascism. The political parties of the left were more successful at the local level than they were at the national level. Local government was able to pursue an aggressive economic programme and retain a degree of insulation from interest group politics by creating a range of extra- and inter-firm institutions in such areas as productive associations, industrial parks, financial and marketing consortia, and collective service centres (Best 1992, 203-221).

22. This area is presently the subject of a major research programme sponsored by the National Economic and Social Council, entitled The Determinants of Competitive Advantage in Selected Irish Sectors, that is being carried out by the Graduate School of Business, University College Dublin, in association with the Economic and Social Research Institute and Professor Michael Best of the University of Massachusetts, Lowell.

23. The strength of any such EMU would place severe constraints on UK fiscal and monetary policy. However, the European Union has yet to evolve the type of fiscal transfer mechanisms that permit the individual States of the US to function comfortably within such a full fiscal and monetary union. Hence, the scope for destabilizing UK-Irish policy differences might be greater than one might suspect.

24. We do not form any judgement on the economic wisdom of the UK deviating from evolving EU policy norms. In a situation where the British economy continues to dominate economic activity in Northern Ireland (to a much greater extent than it influences activity in the Republic of Ireland), the North is able to insulate itself partially from world economic shocks by staying within

the UK fiscal union. However, it is a moot point if such a policy will serve British economic policy-makers' interests in their efforts to insulate the entire UK economy from world economic shocks and to promote long-term growth.

25. Asymmetric shocks are of a type that bear heavily on one region and not on others. Thus, for example, a decline in the textiles industry would affect Northern Ireland much more severely than it would affect regions in the South of England, simply because of the dominance of the textiles sector in the North.

26. It should be pointed out that negotiations leading to EMU are attempting to deal with the 'free rider' issue of member States that opt out. Hence, it is likely that some form of economic sanction will be put in place to deter competitive devaluations and other economically disruptive actions by the non-members of EMU.

27. See section 6.2 for a treatment of the likely future of the reformed CAP.

APPENDIX — NORTH-SOUTH ECONOMIC RESEARCH

1. The high natural rate of population growth was another factor driving up the labour supply and, other things being equal, increasing unemployment. However, what is of relevance in the Barry and Bradley (1990) study is the change in the natural rate over the relevant period 1979-87. Migration and labour force participation mechanisms were modelled behaviourally, if somewhat crudely, and are not independent explanatory factors, but simply respond to external and policy shocks.

2. For a survey of earlier modelling work in the South, see Bradley and Fanning (1981).

JOHN BRADLEY is an economist and Research Professor at the Economic and Social Research Institute, Dublin, having previously worked at the Central Bank of Ireland.

He has published widely on the performance of the Irish economy as that of a small peripheral State of the European Union, with a particular focus on adjustment to the single market, the impact of the EU Structural Funds, and the performance of the Irish labour market. From 1992-1995 he directed a joint project on the economies of Ireland, North and South, carried out in association with the Northern Ireland Economic Research Centre, and assisted by a grant from the International Fund for Ireland. Based on the findings of this research, he has edited a book, *The Two Economies of Ireland: Public Policy, Growth and Employment* (1995).

He is also a co-author of two books on the analysis of the small peripheral economies of the European Union (*Stabilization and growth in the EC periphery* (1993) and *Regional aid and convergence* (1995)), and currently directs a trans-EU research collaboration in the development of tools for analysing the economic development of Greece, Ireland, Portugal and Spain.